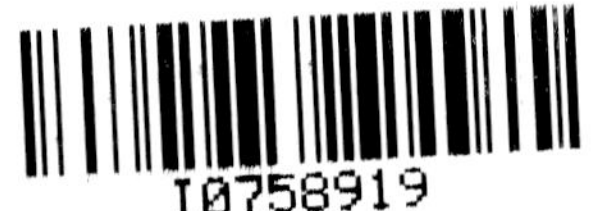

This books belongs to

Color Test Page

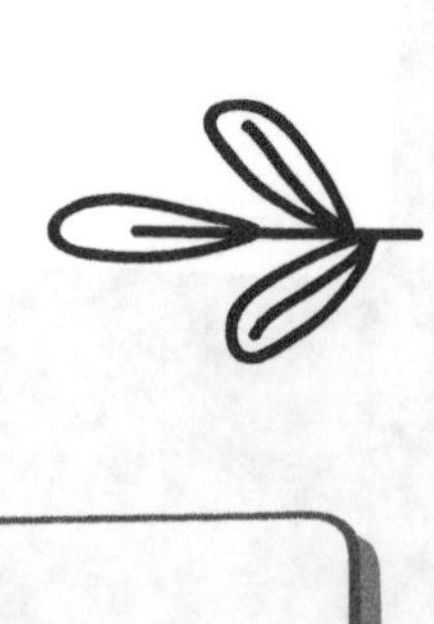
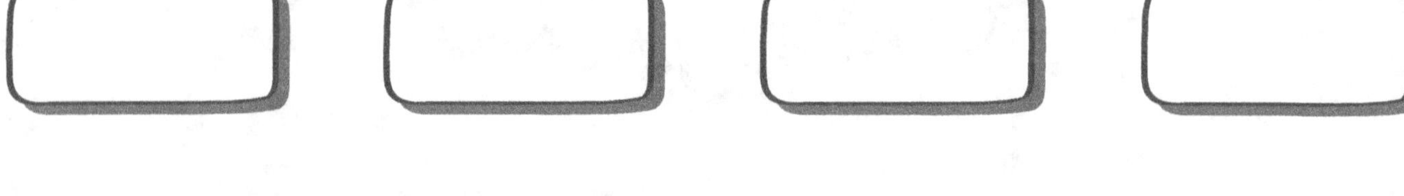
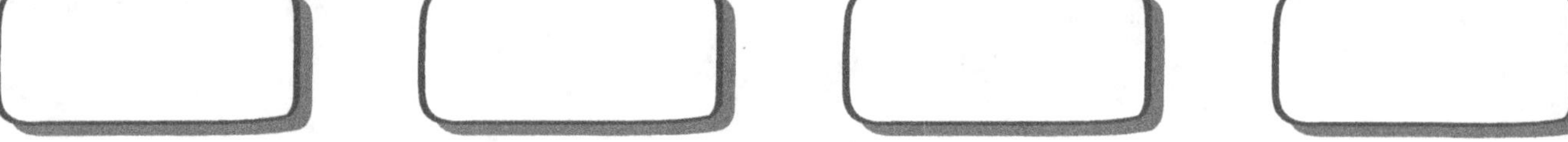

LET'S FIND A PLACE TO GET LOST

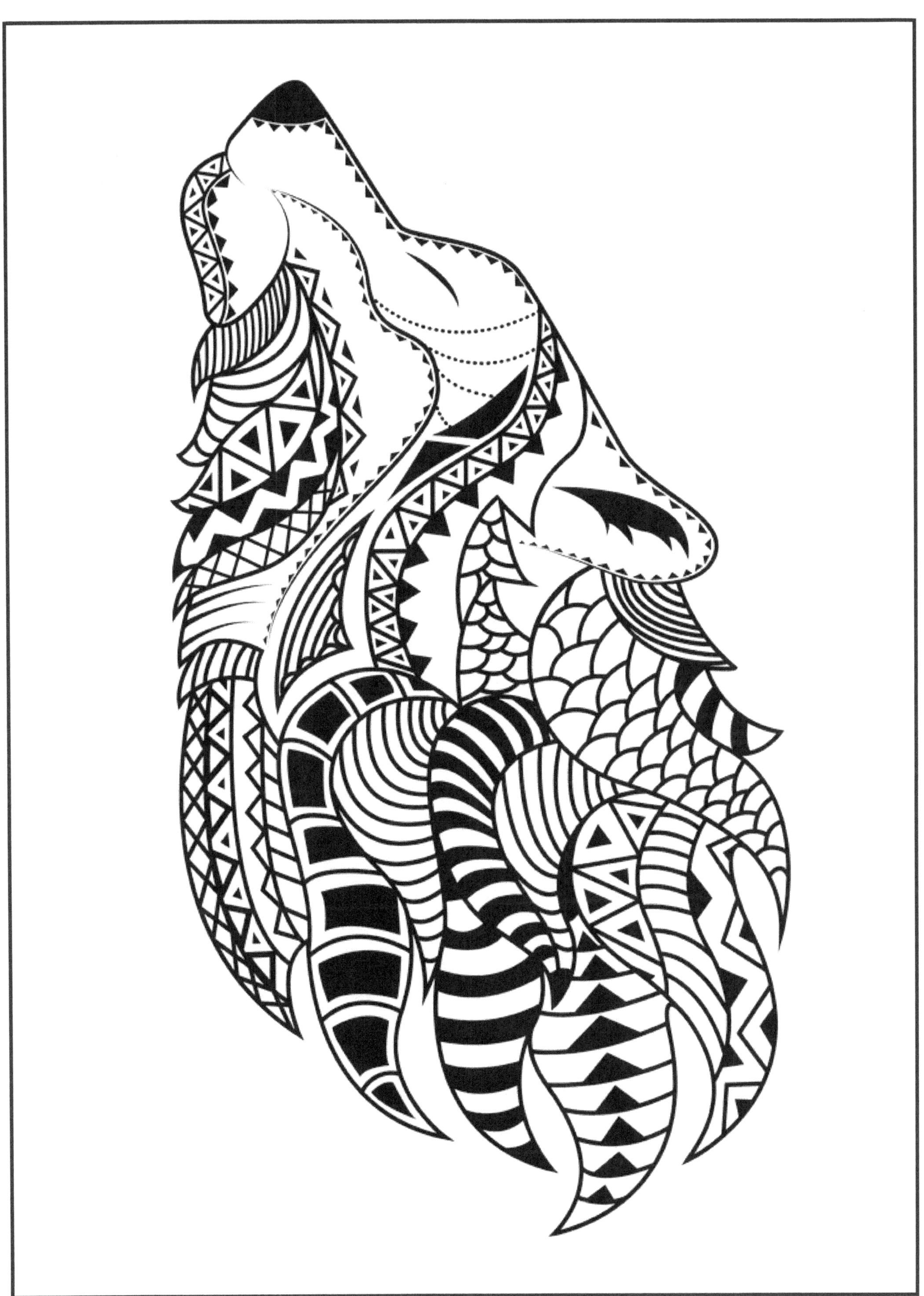

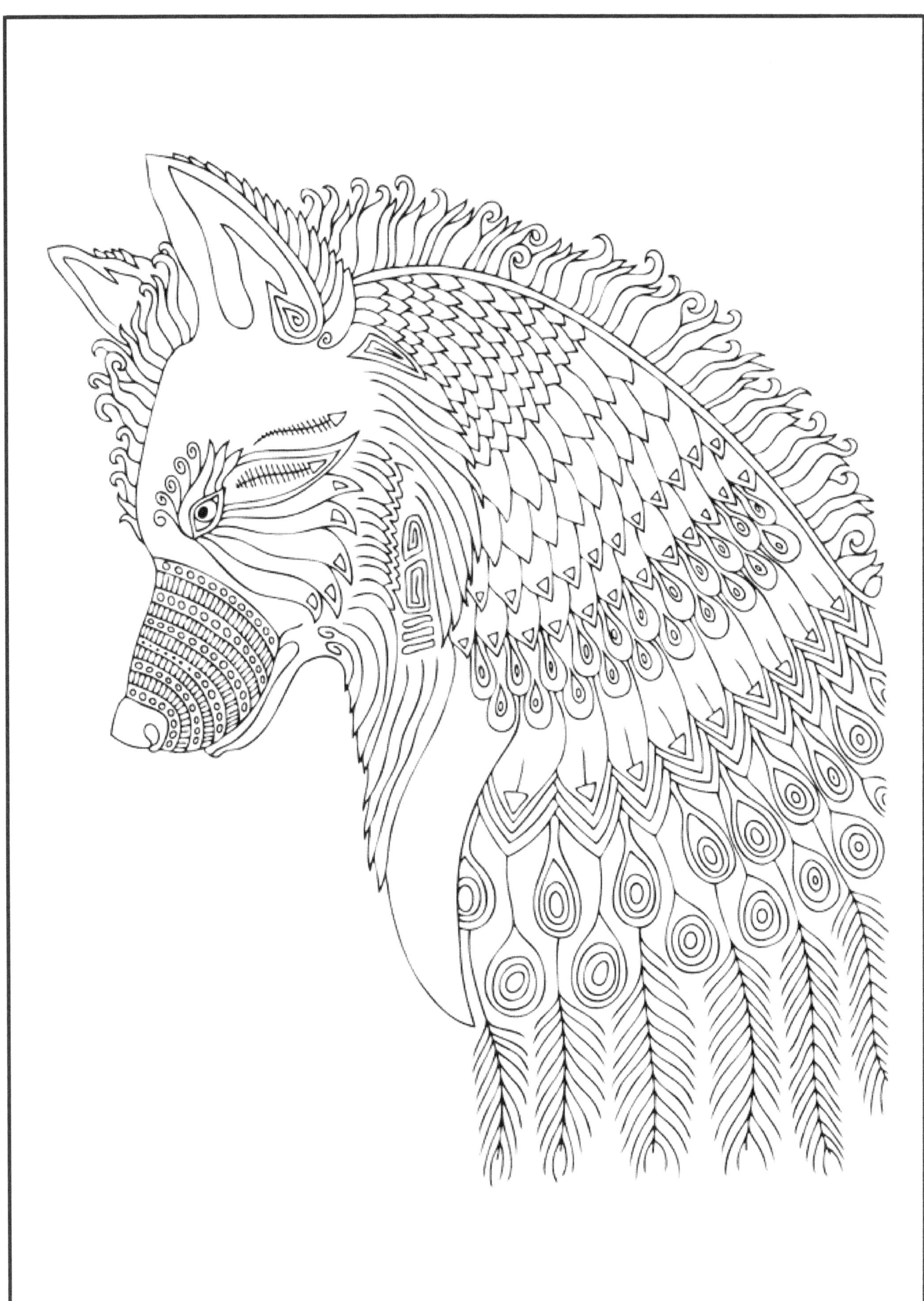

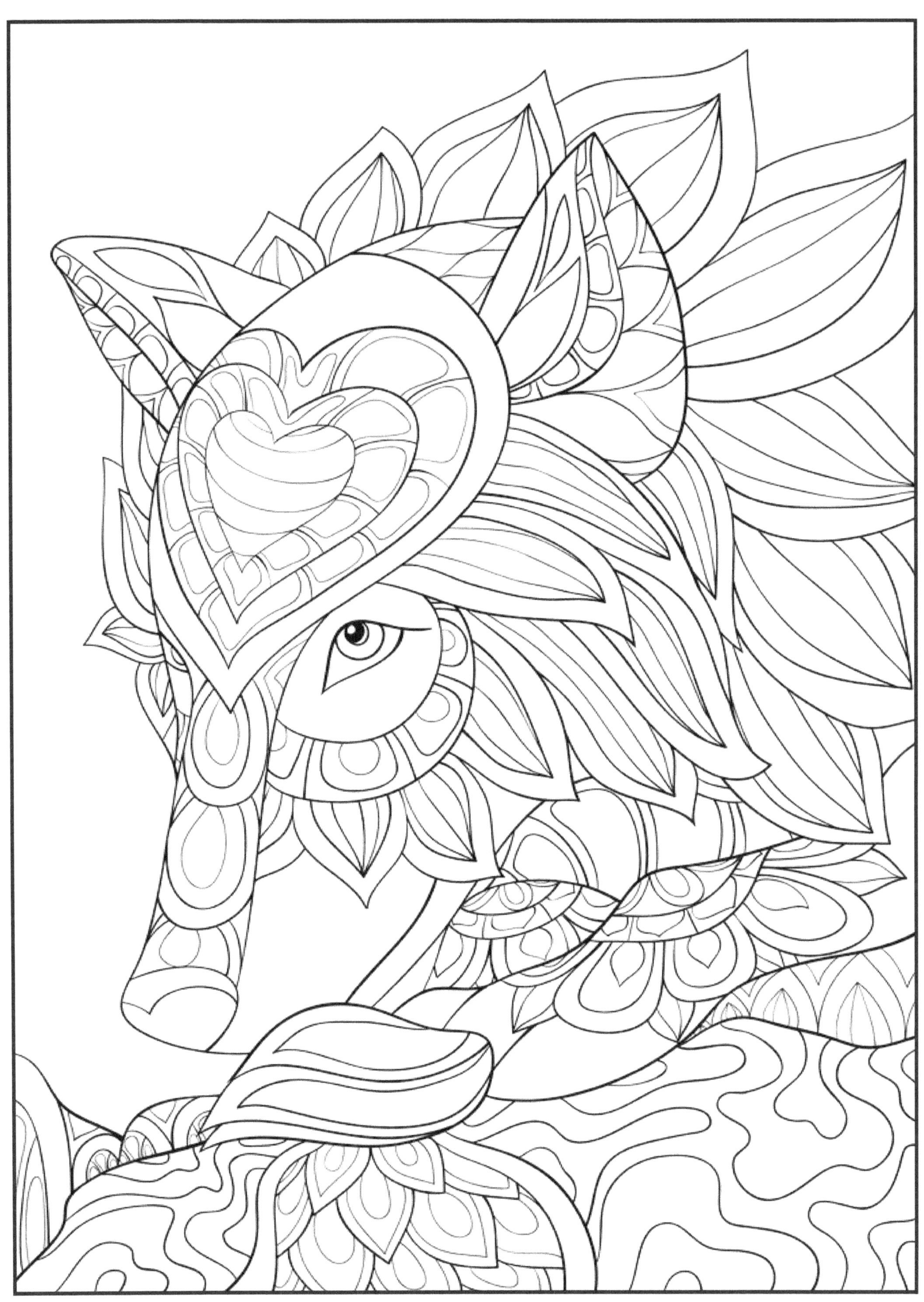

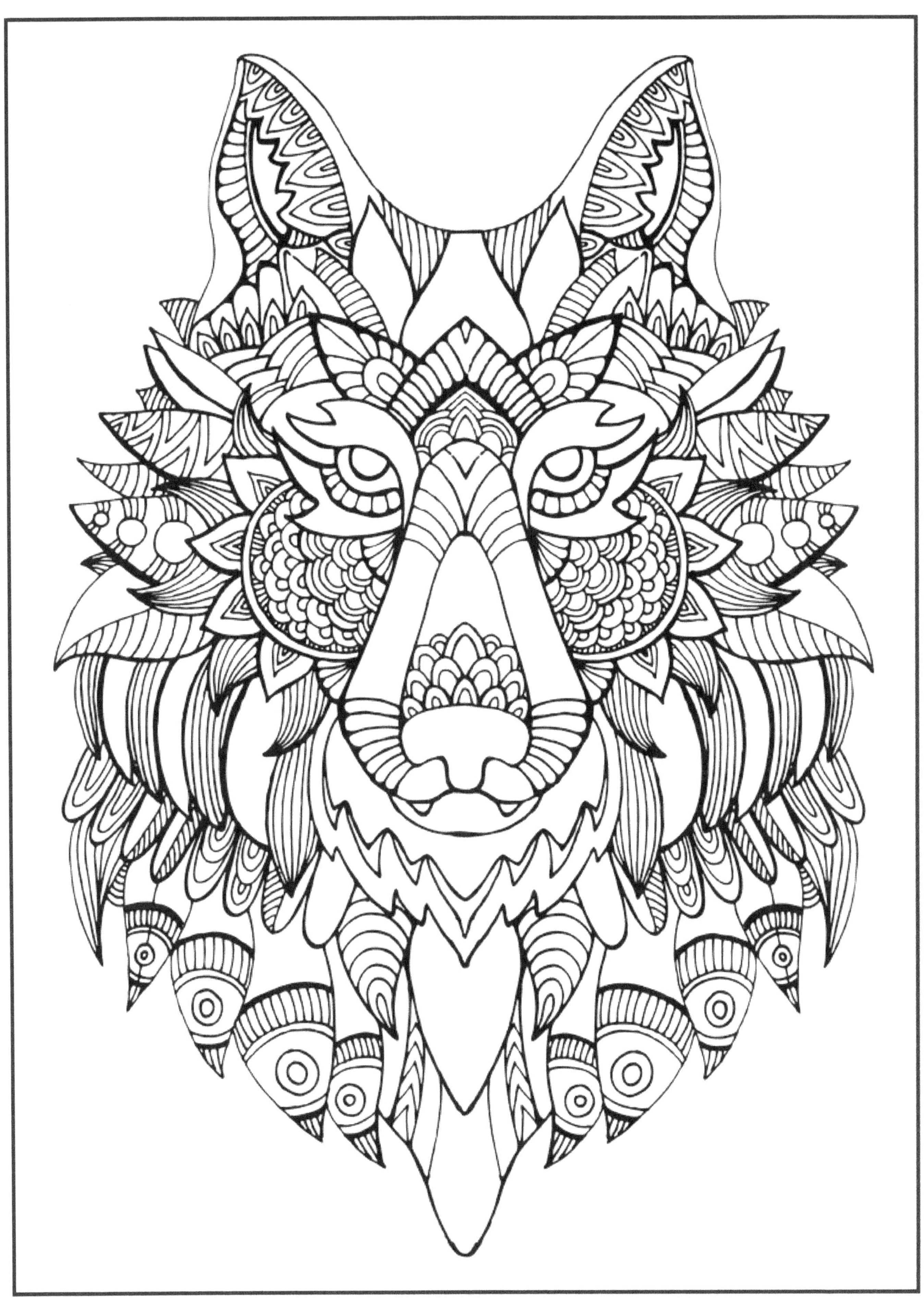

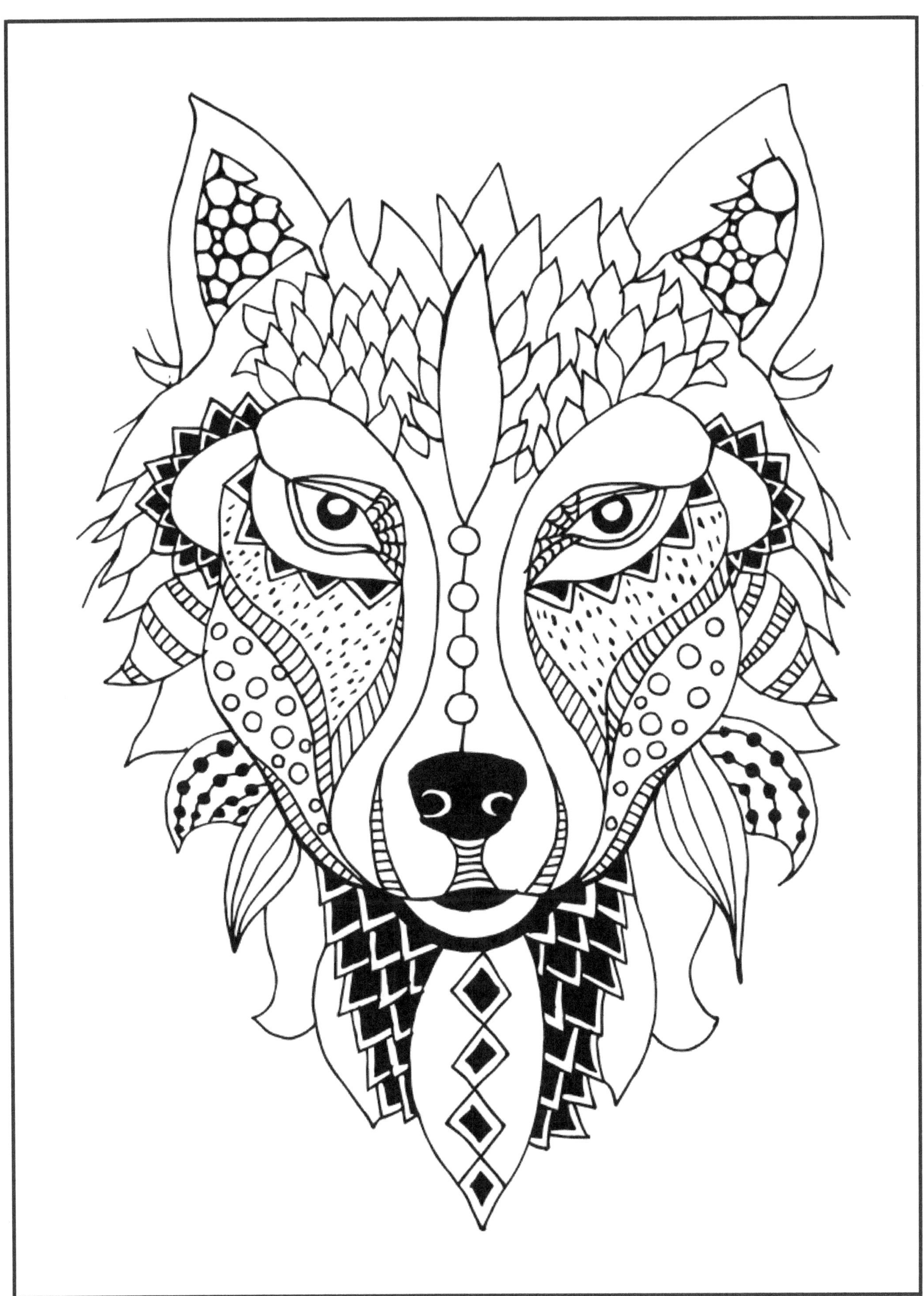

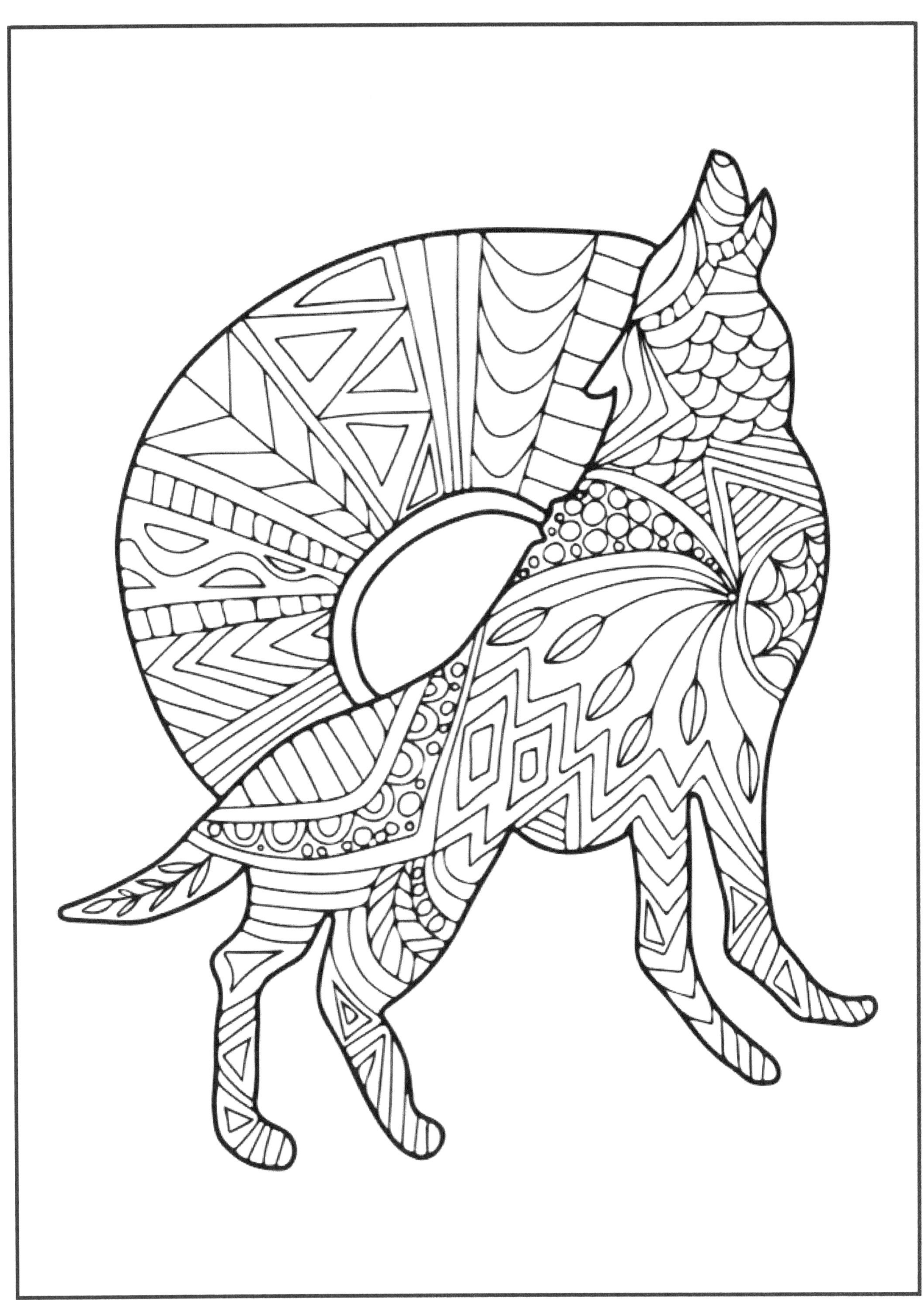

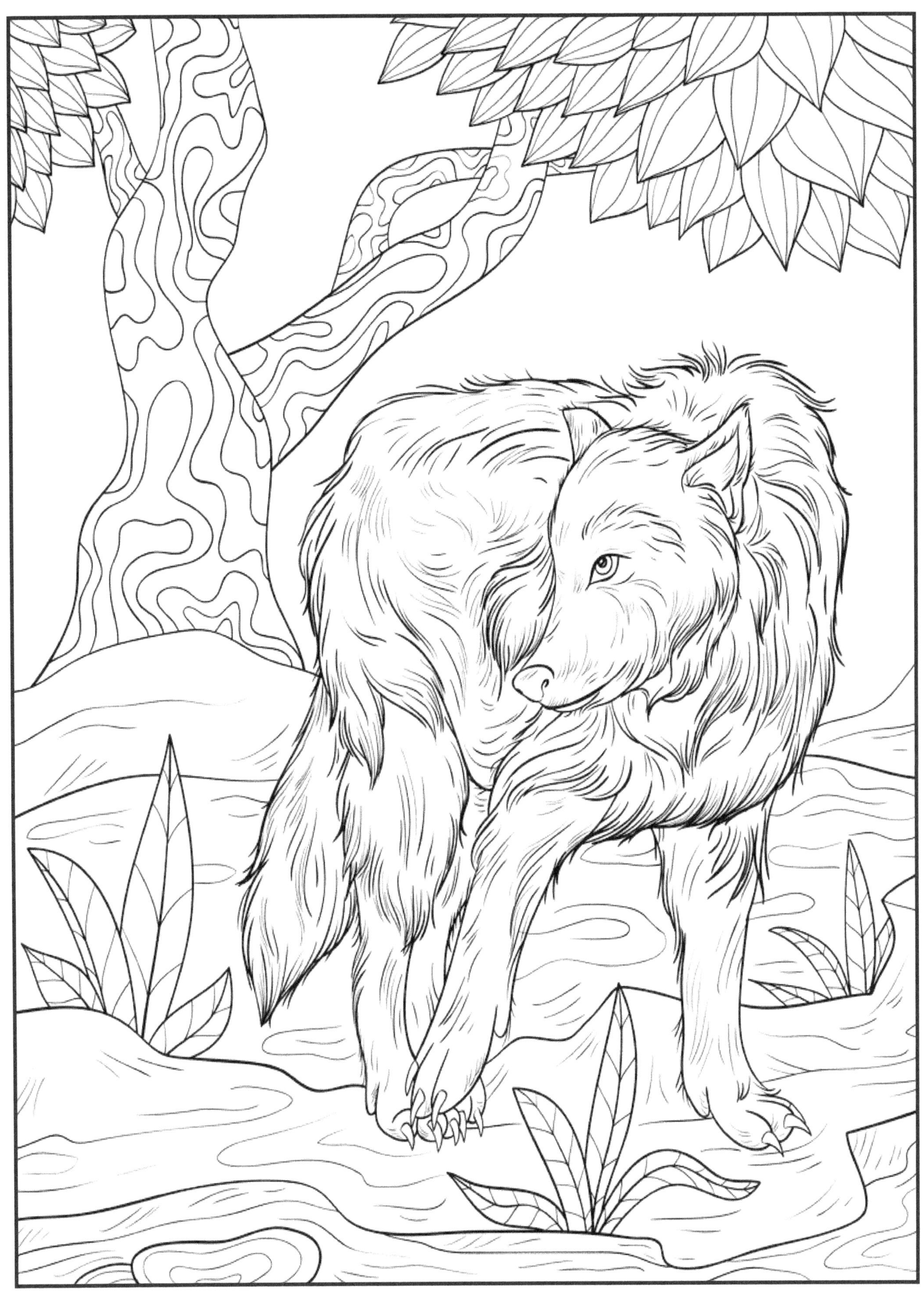

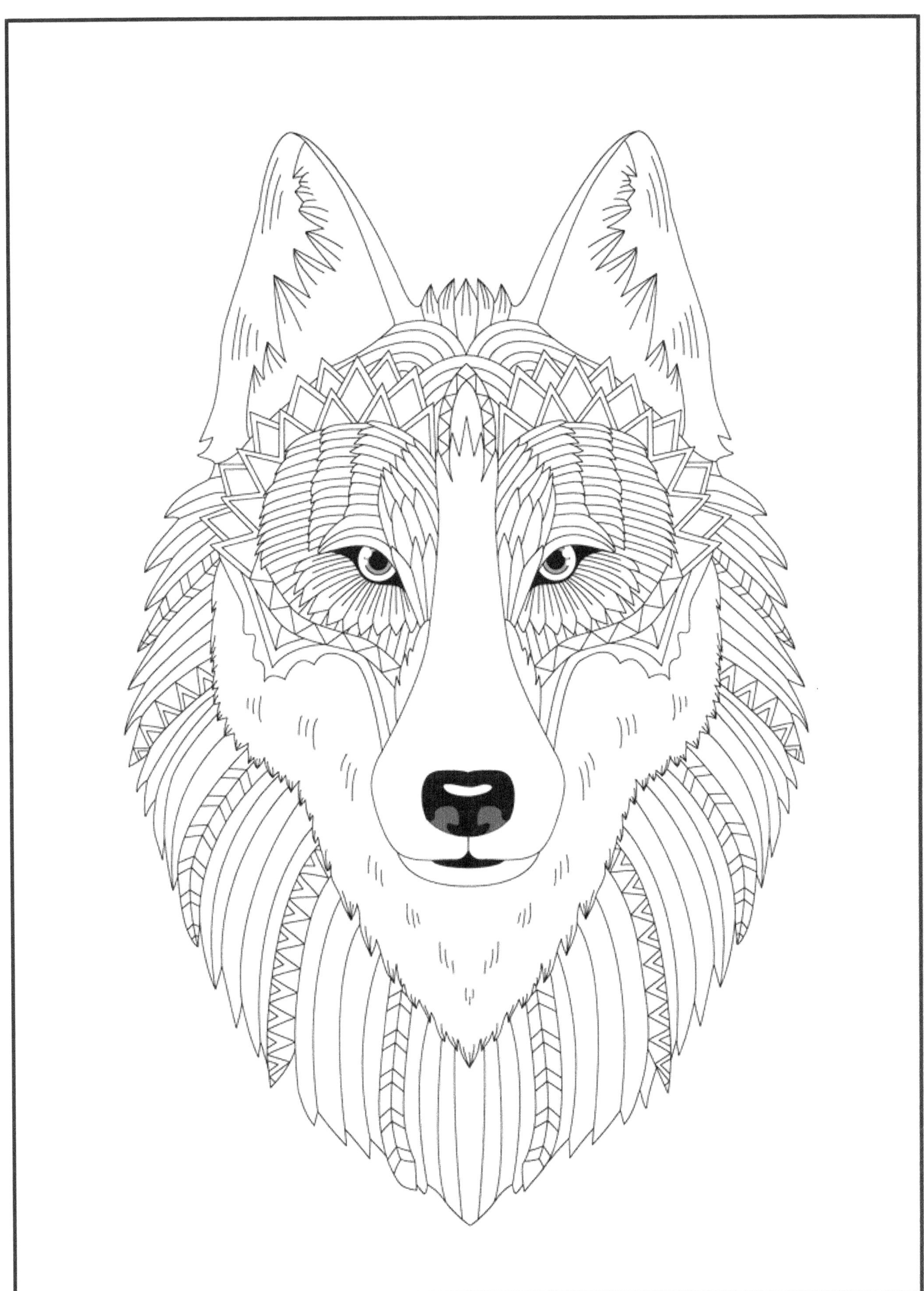

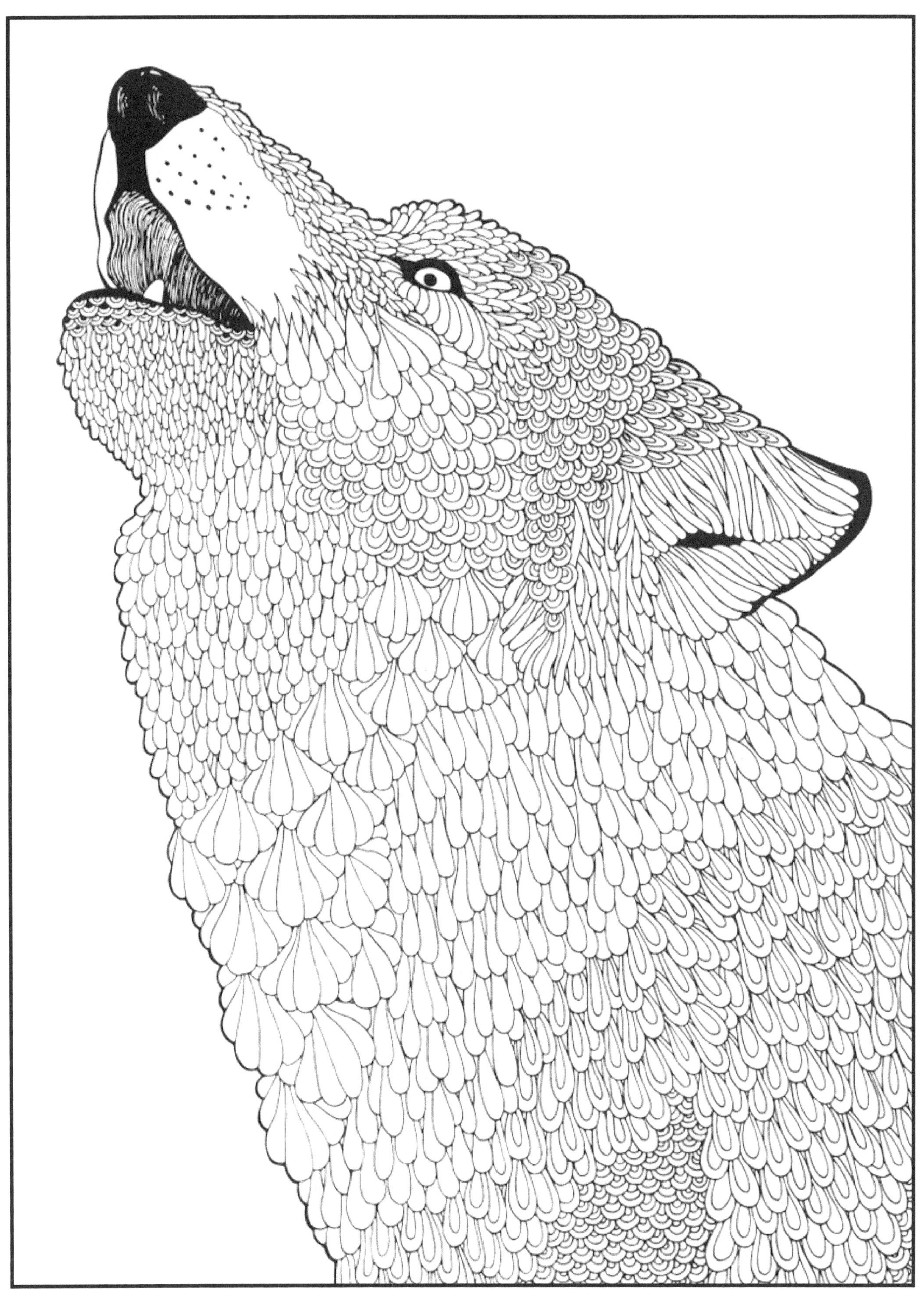

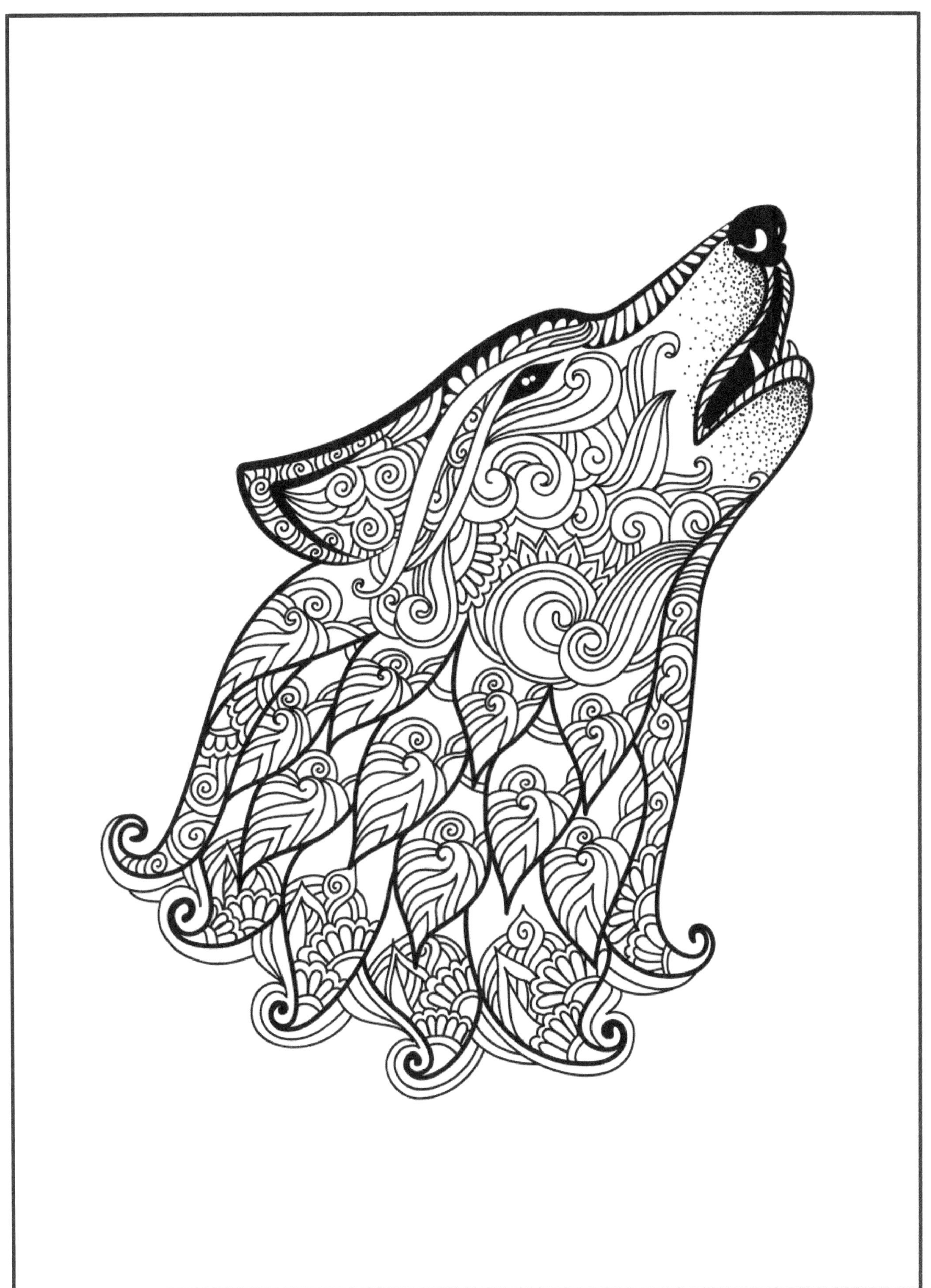

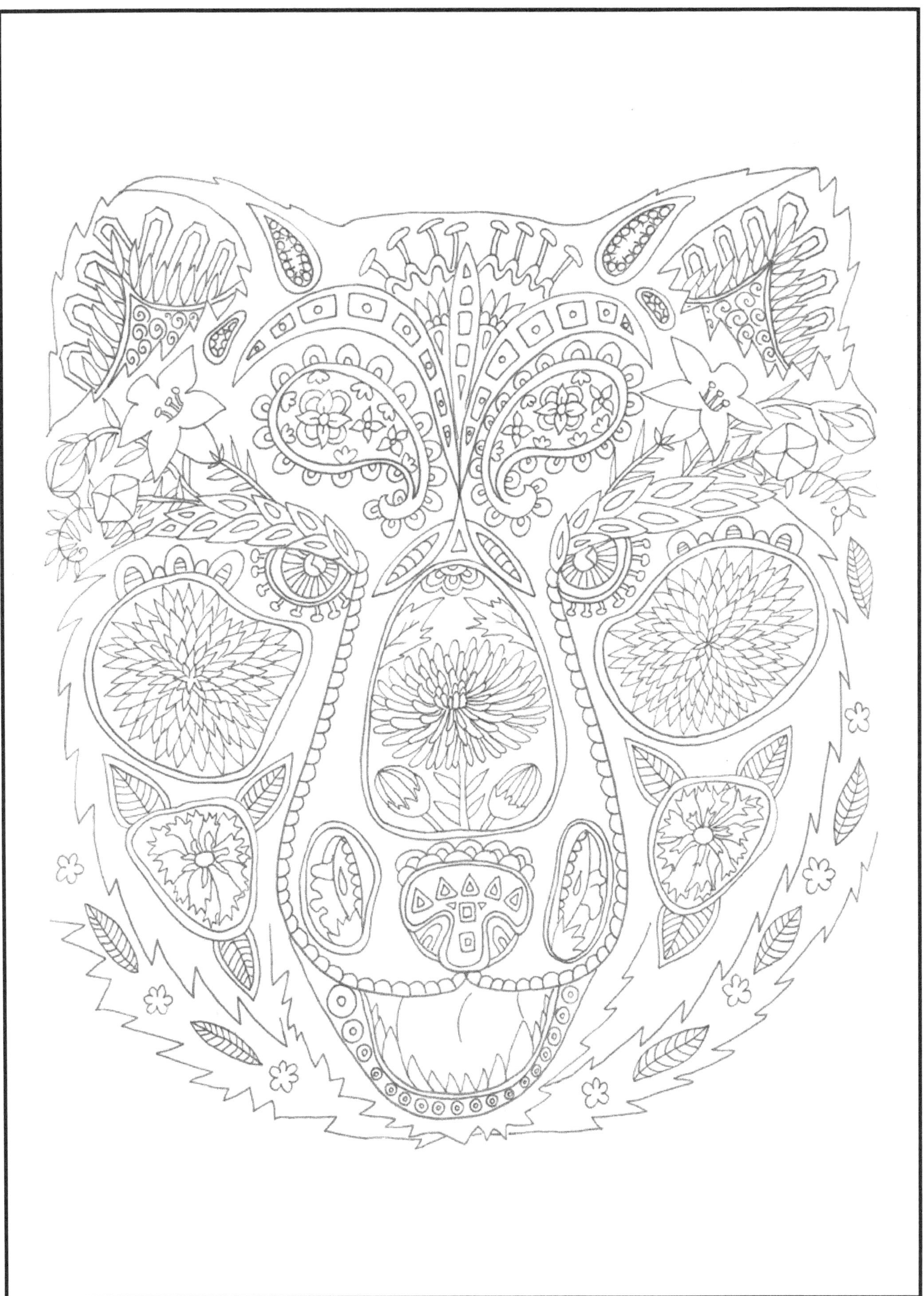

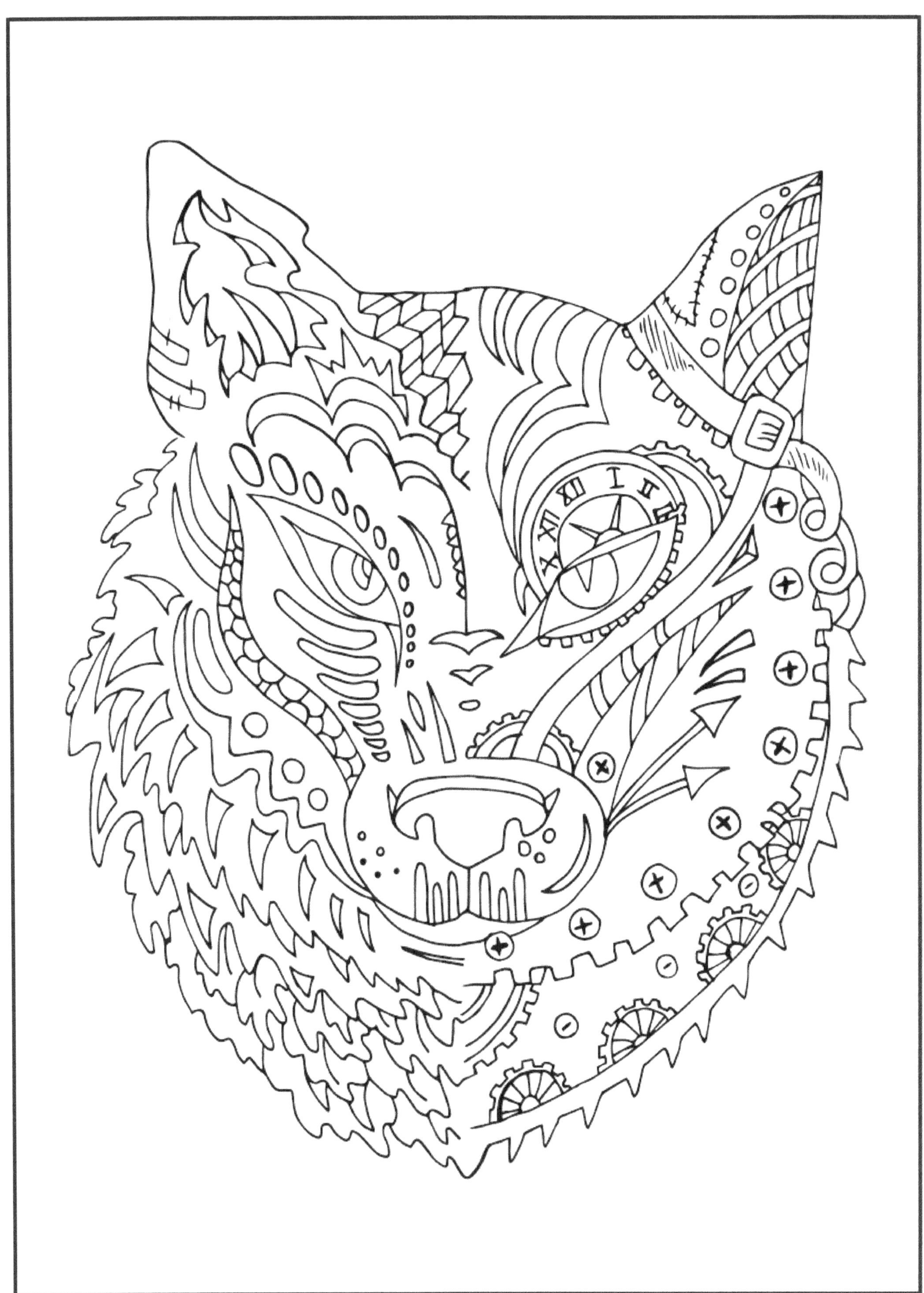

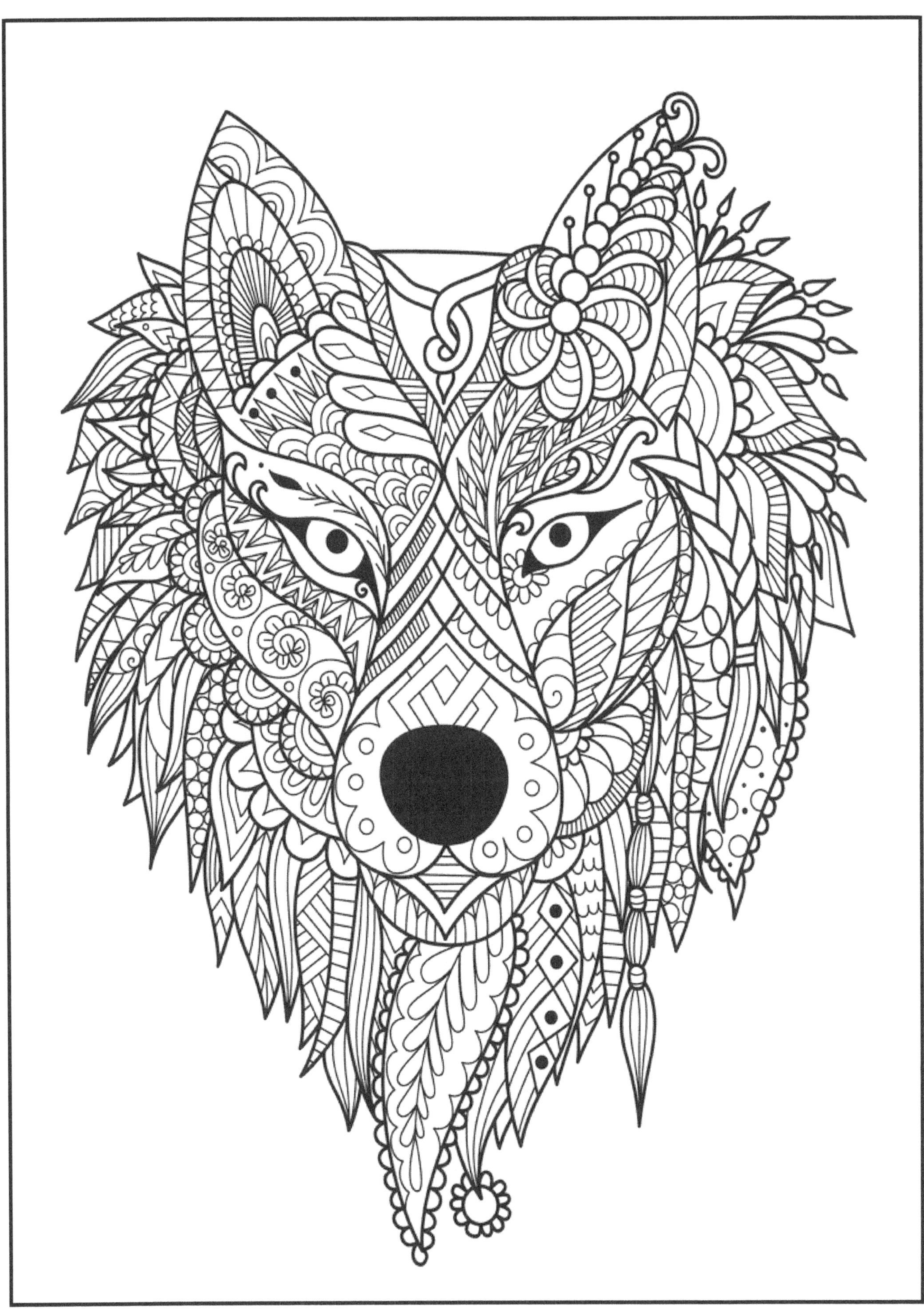

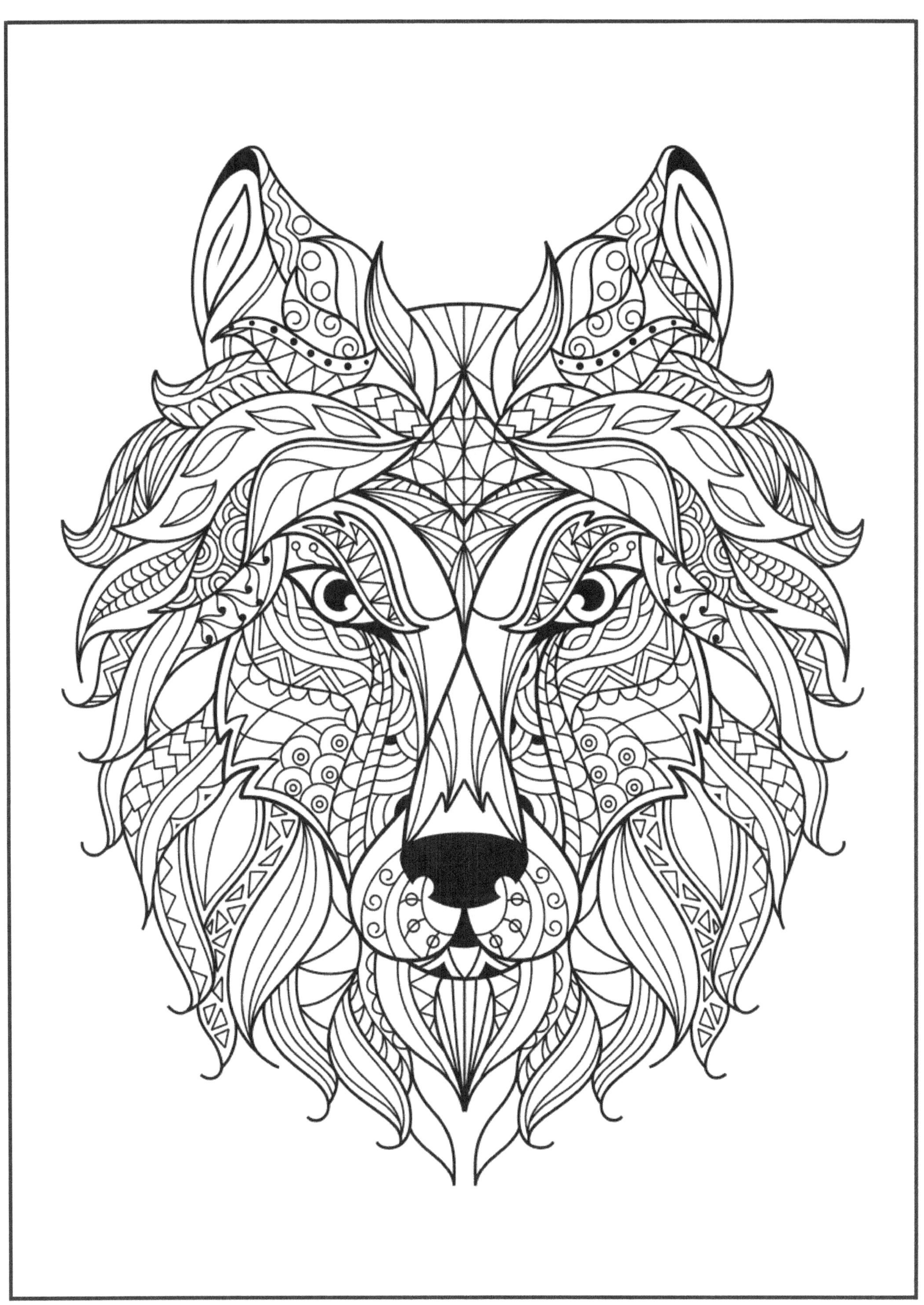

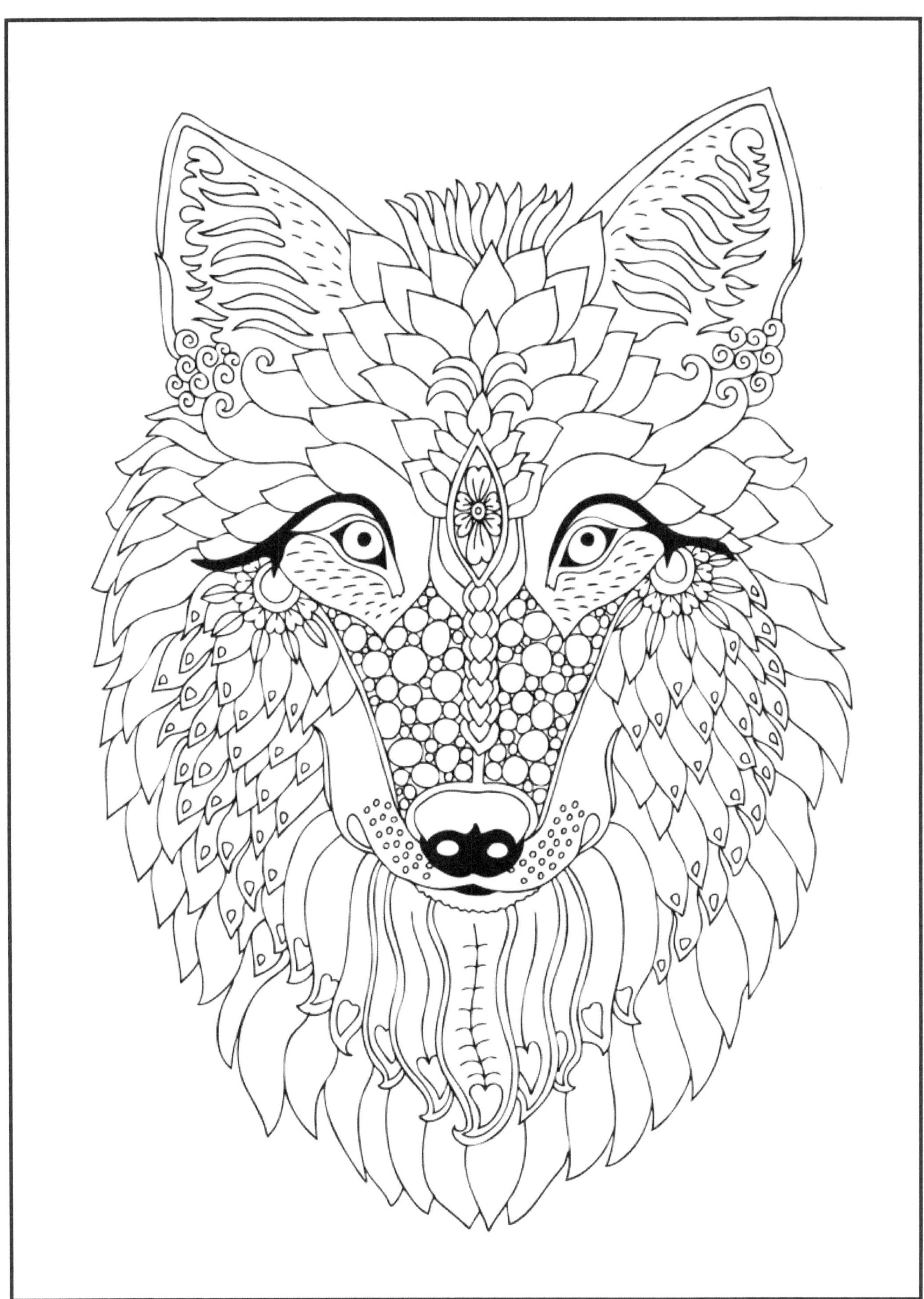

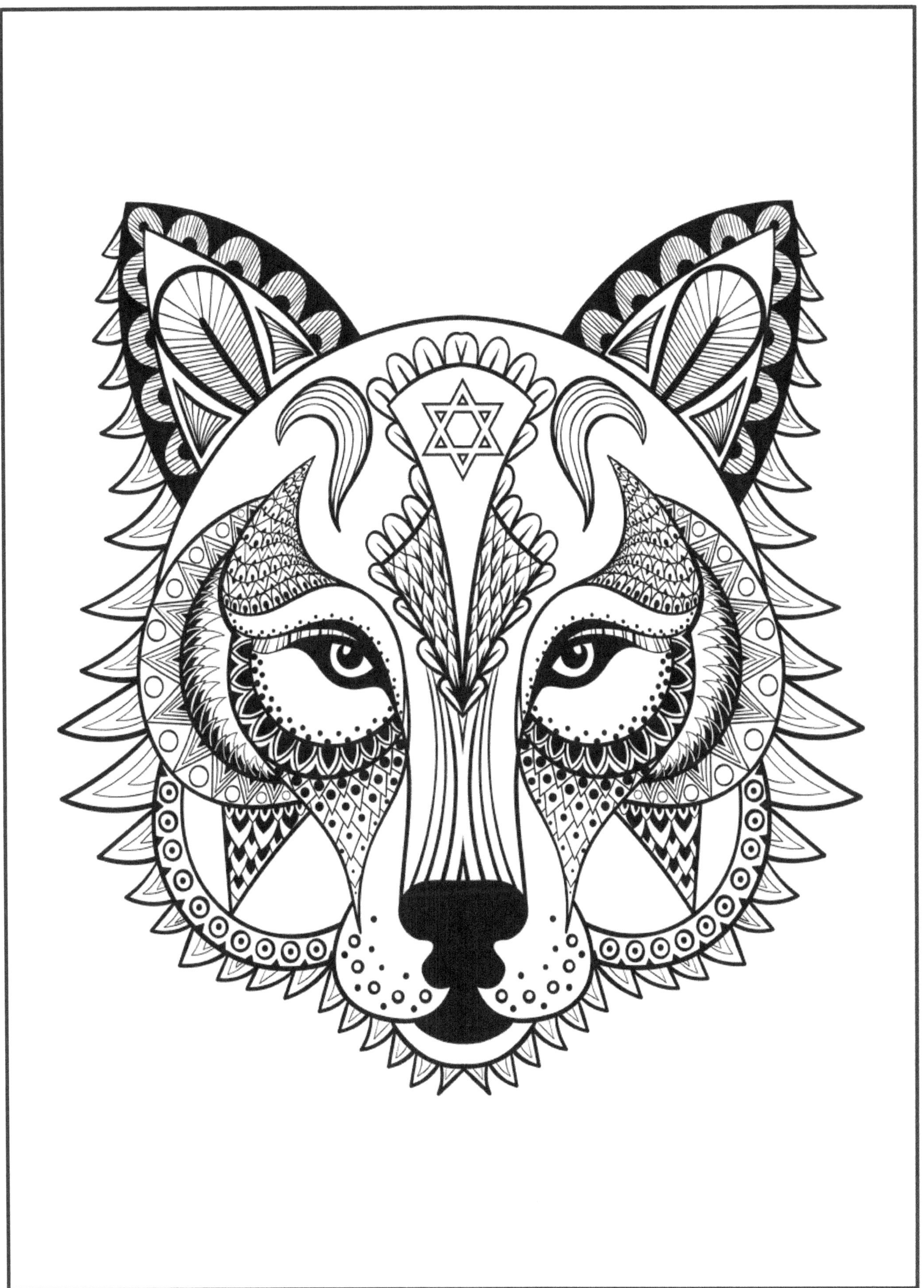

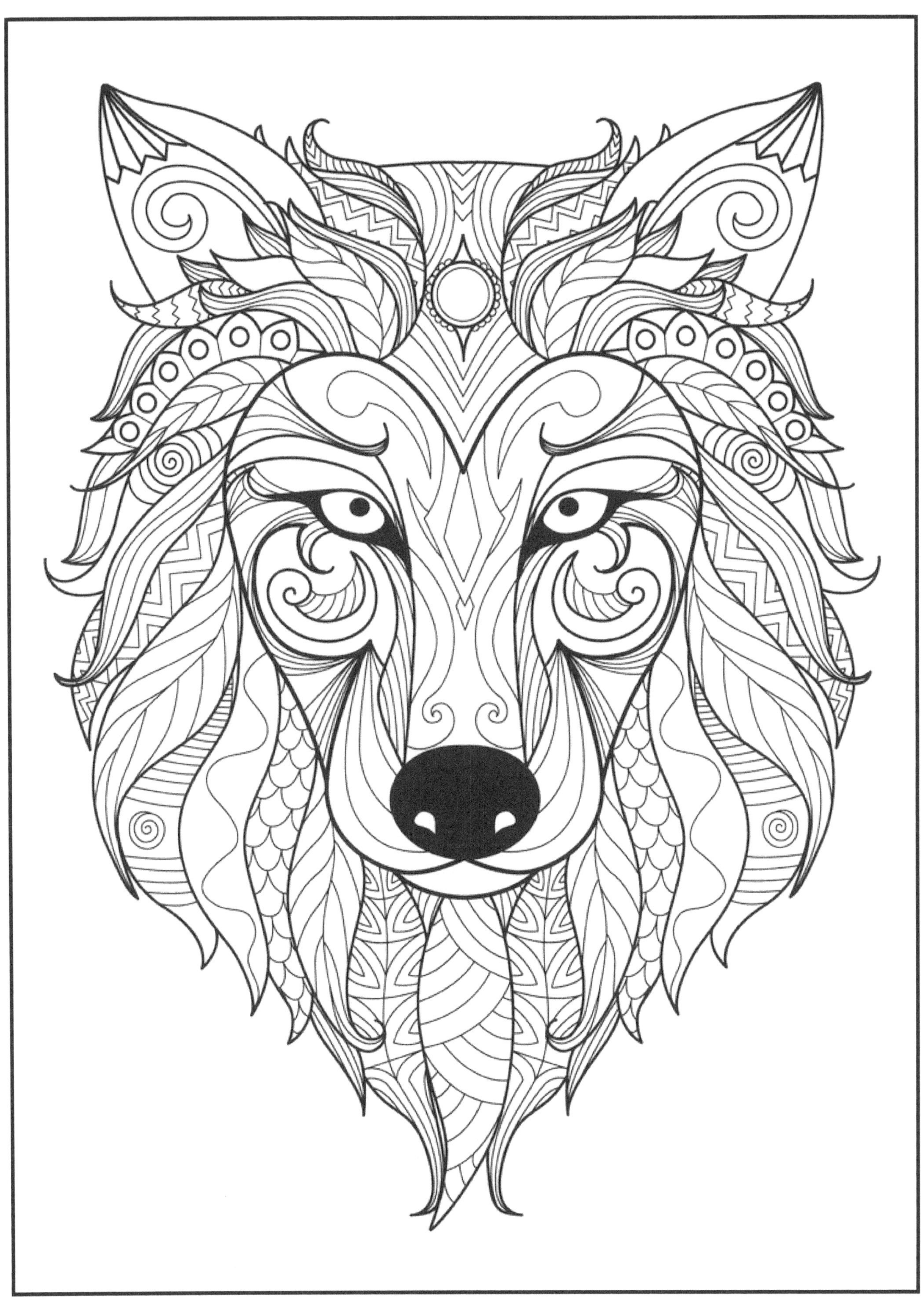

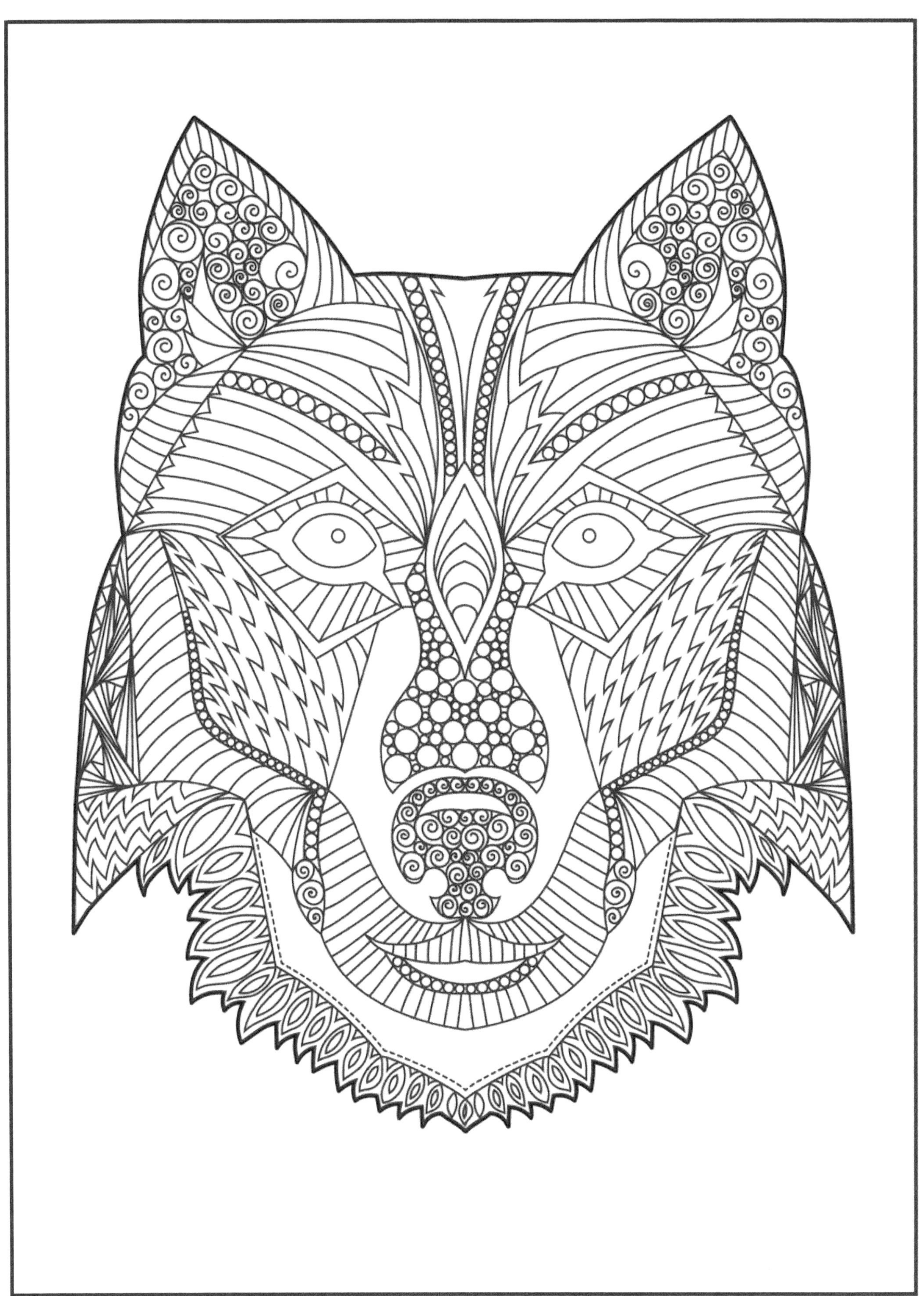

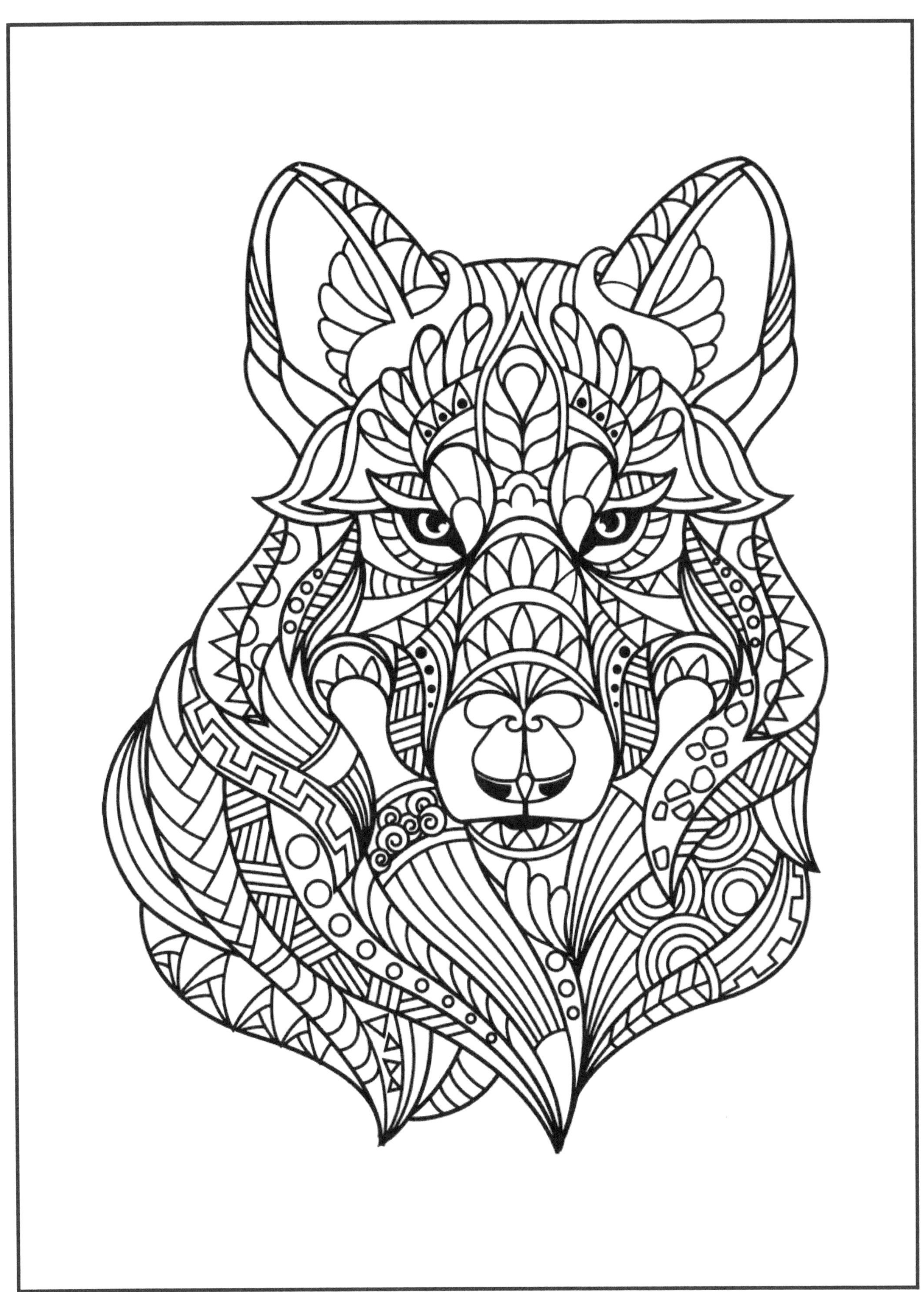

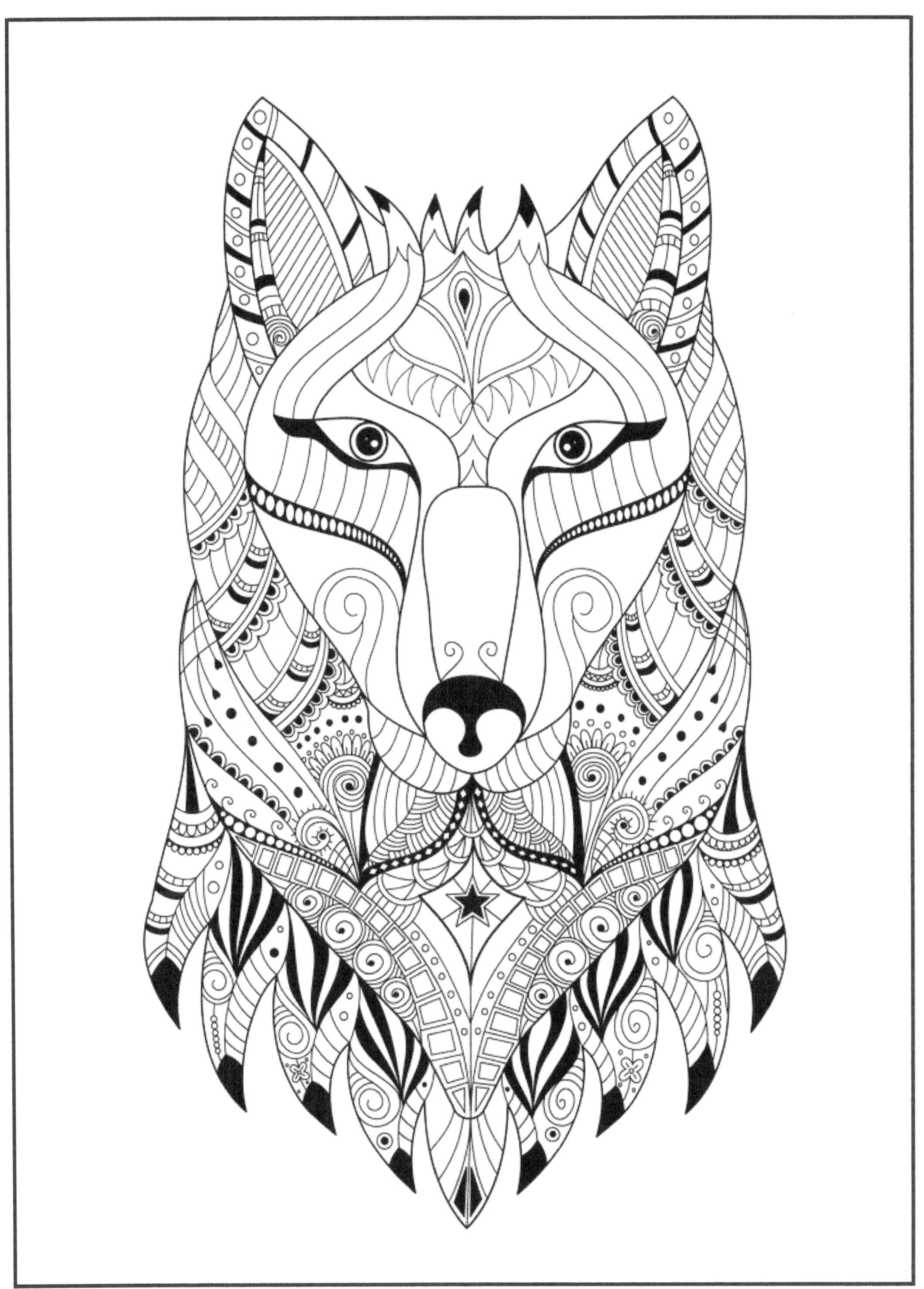

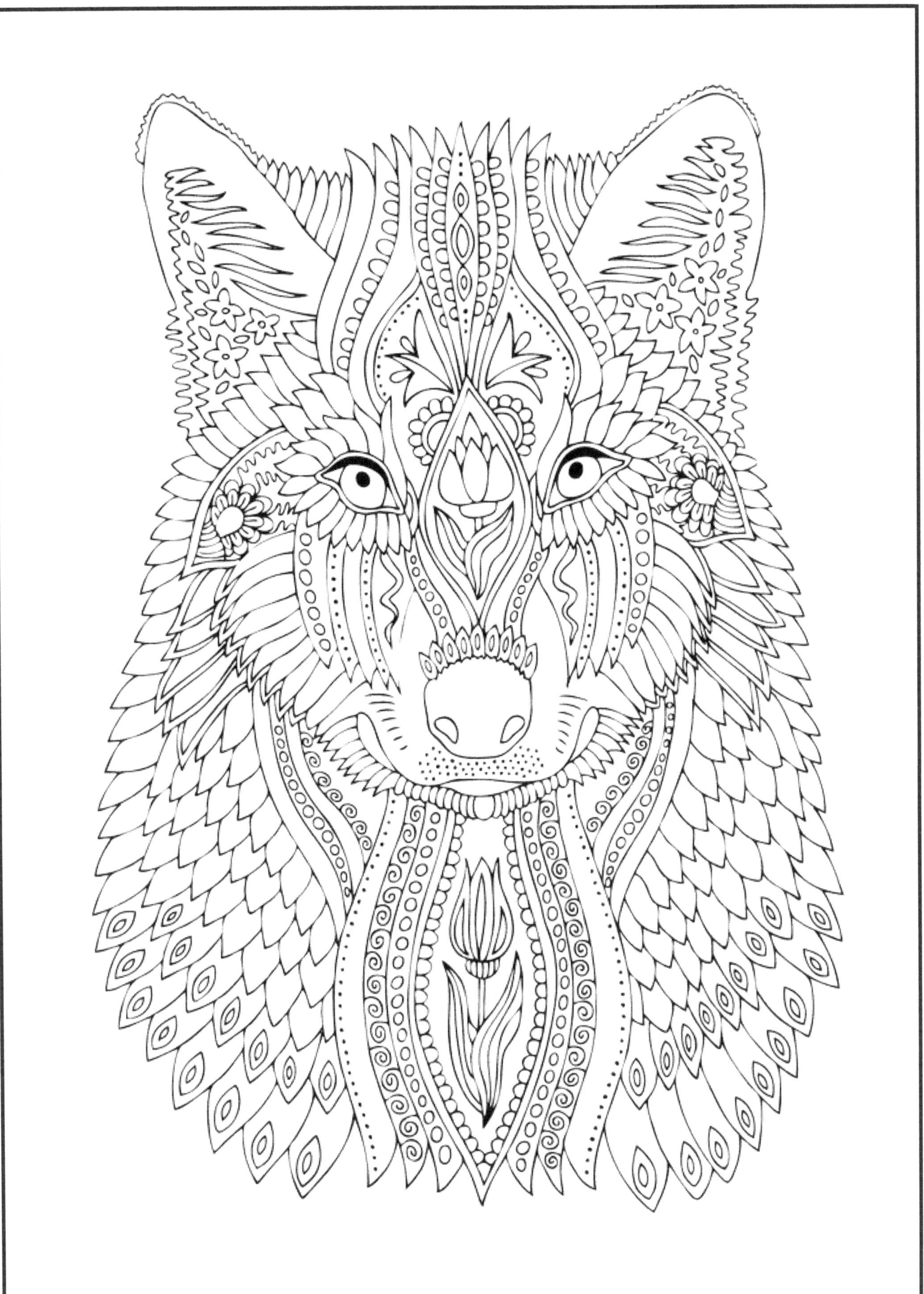

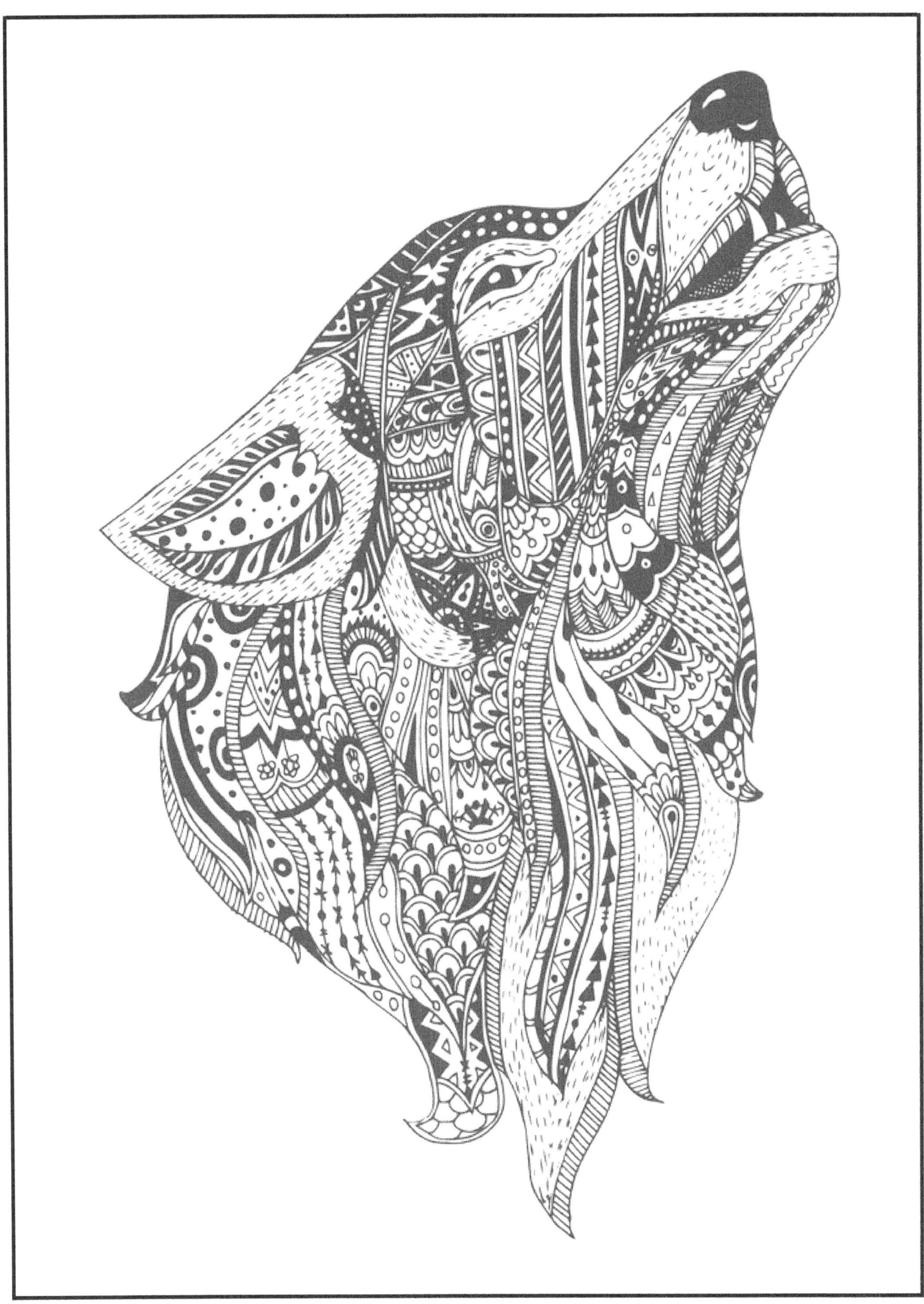

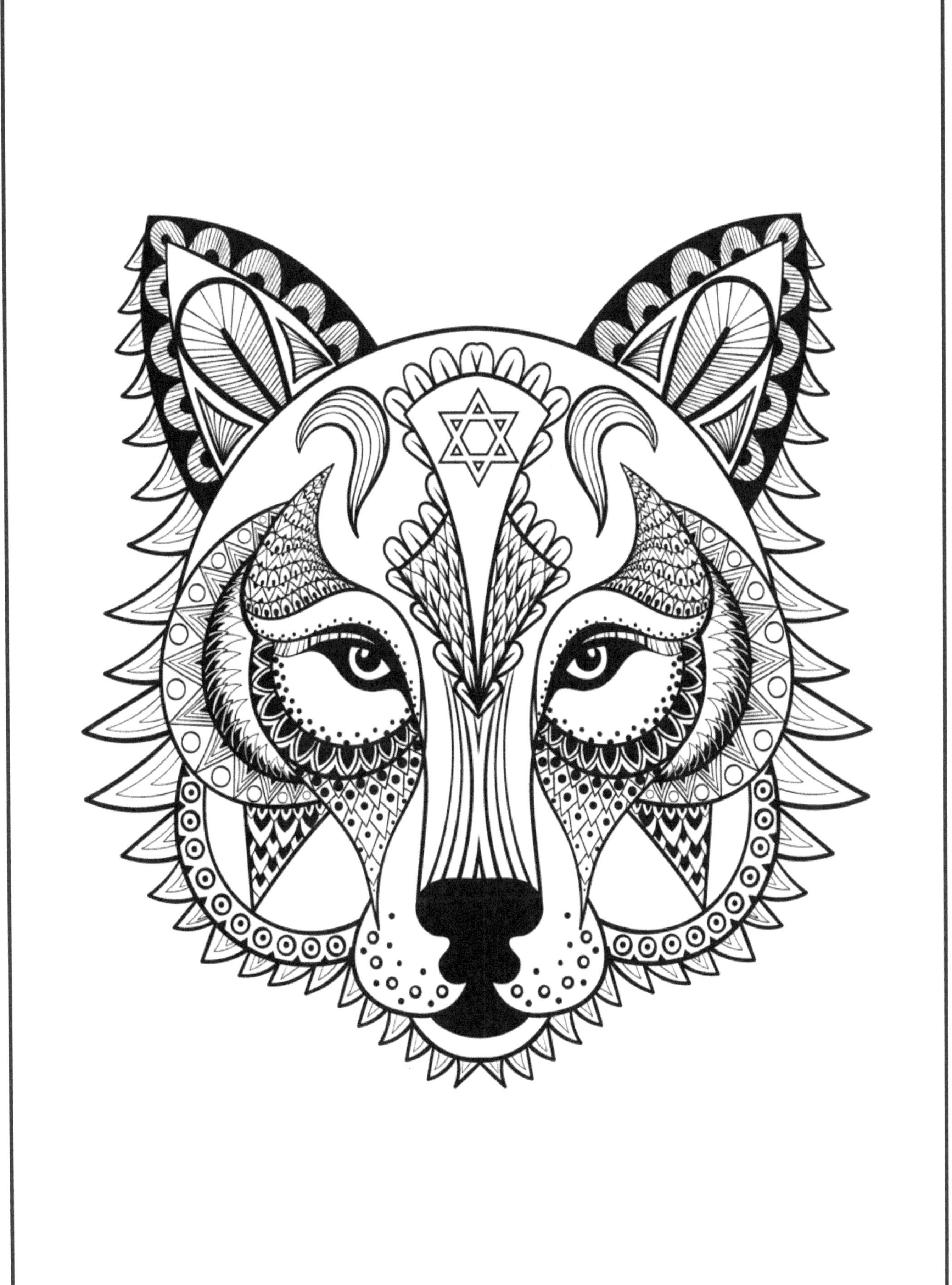

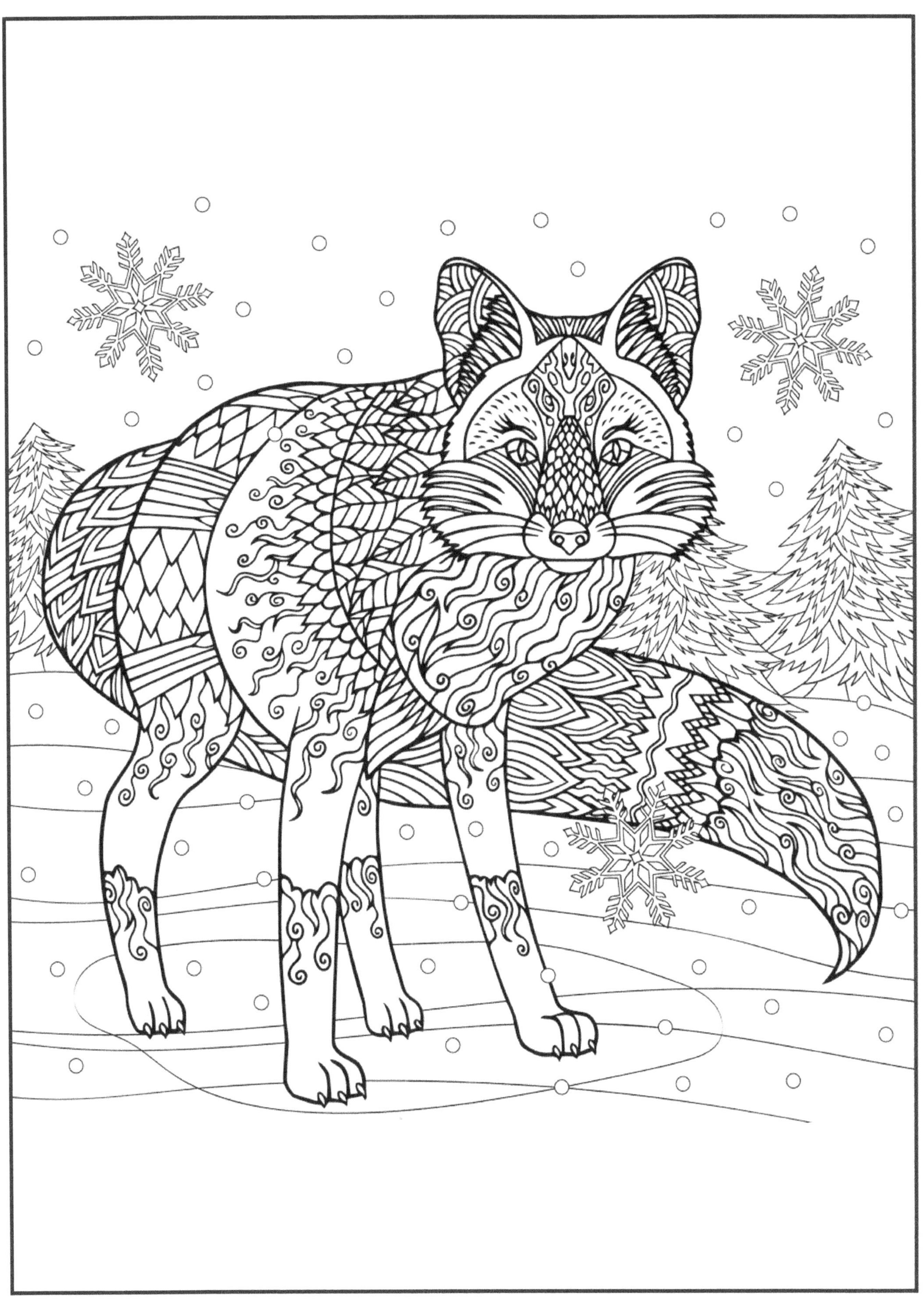

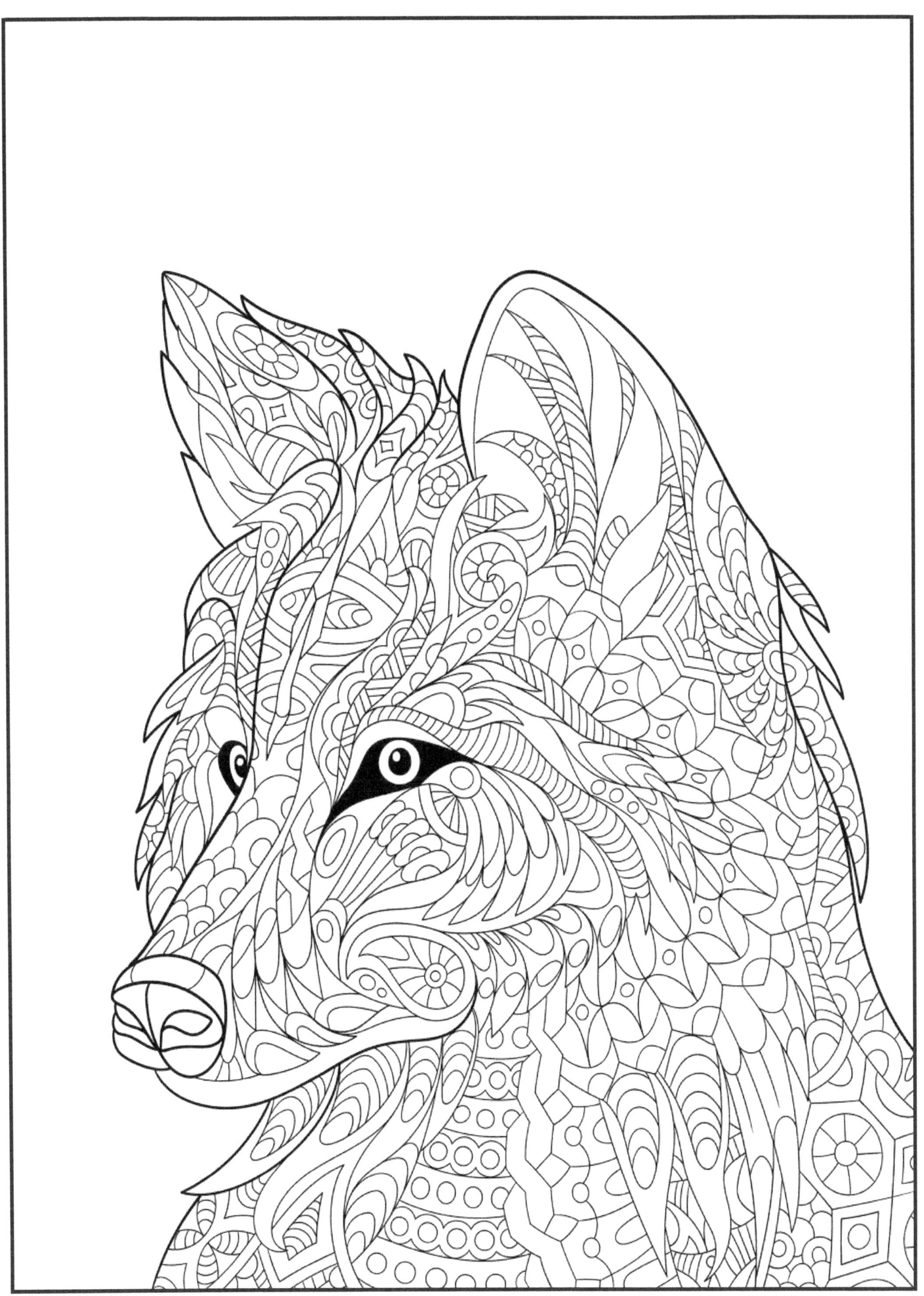

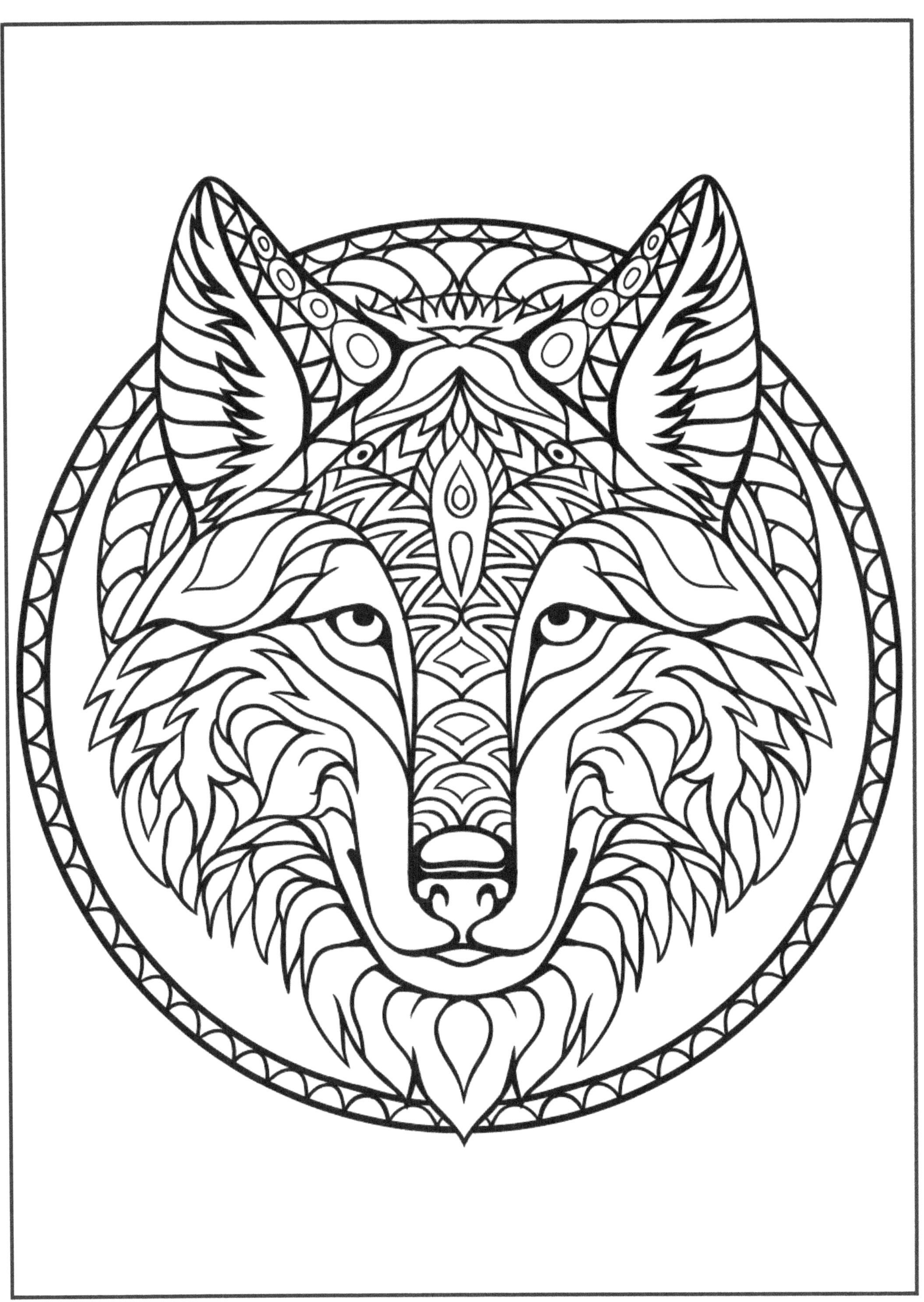

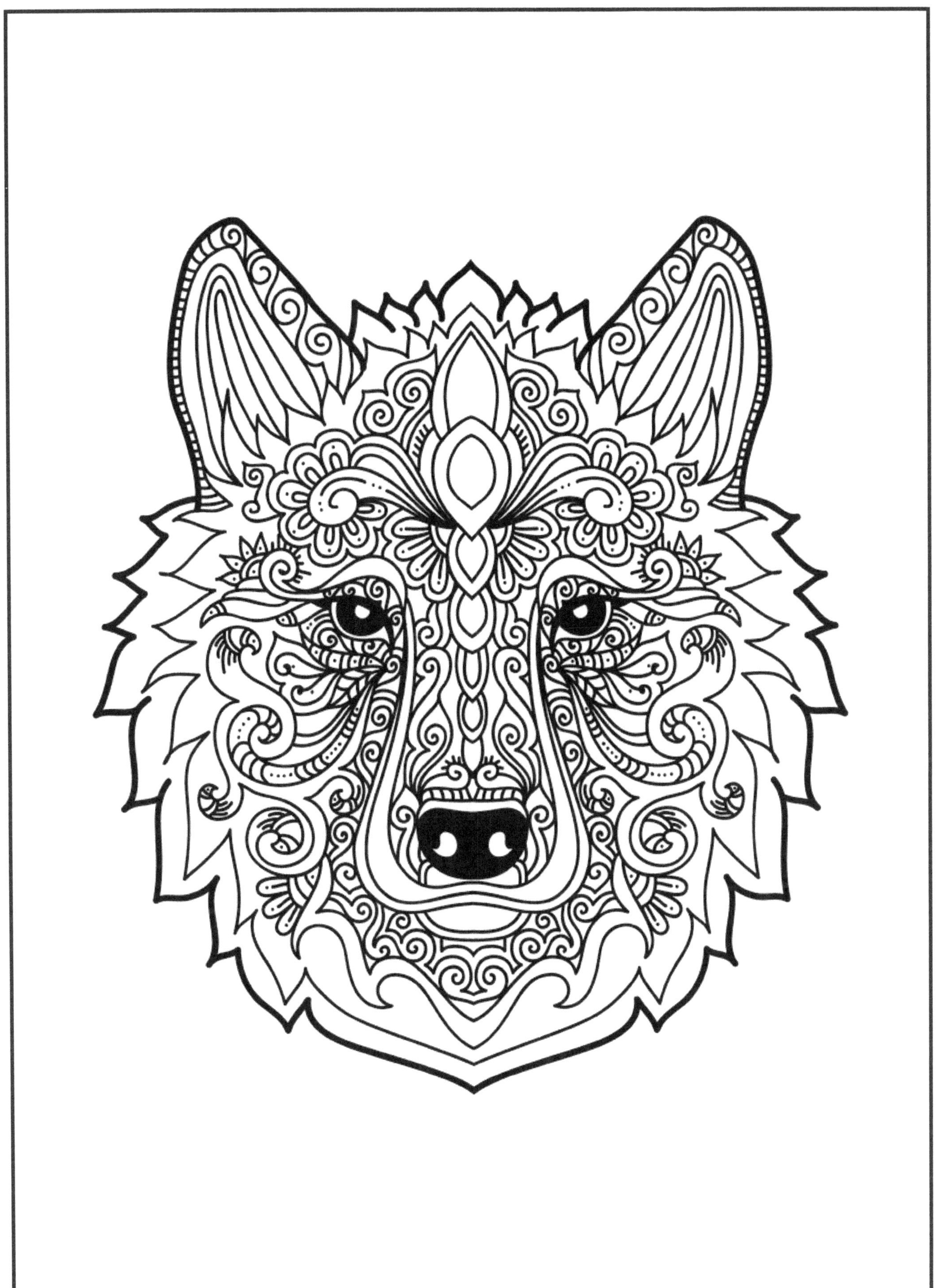

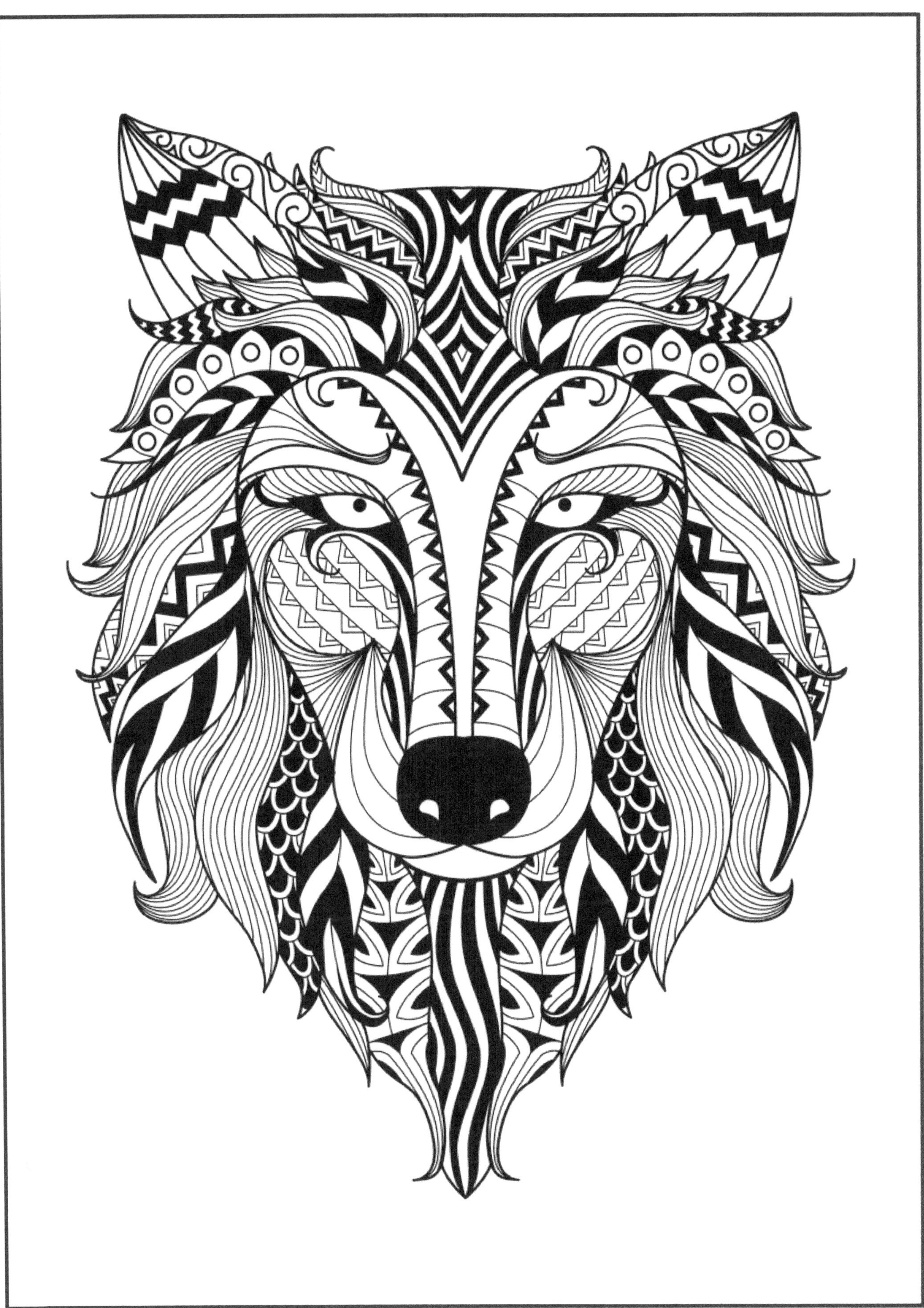

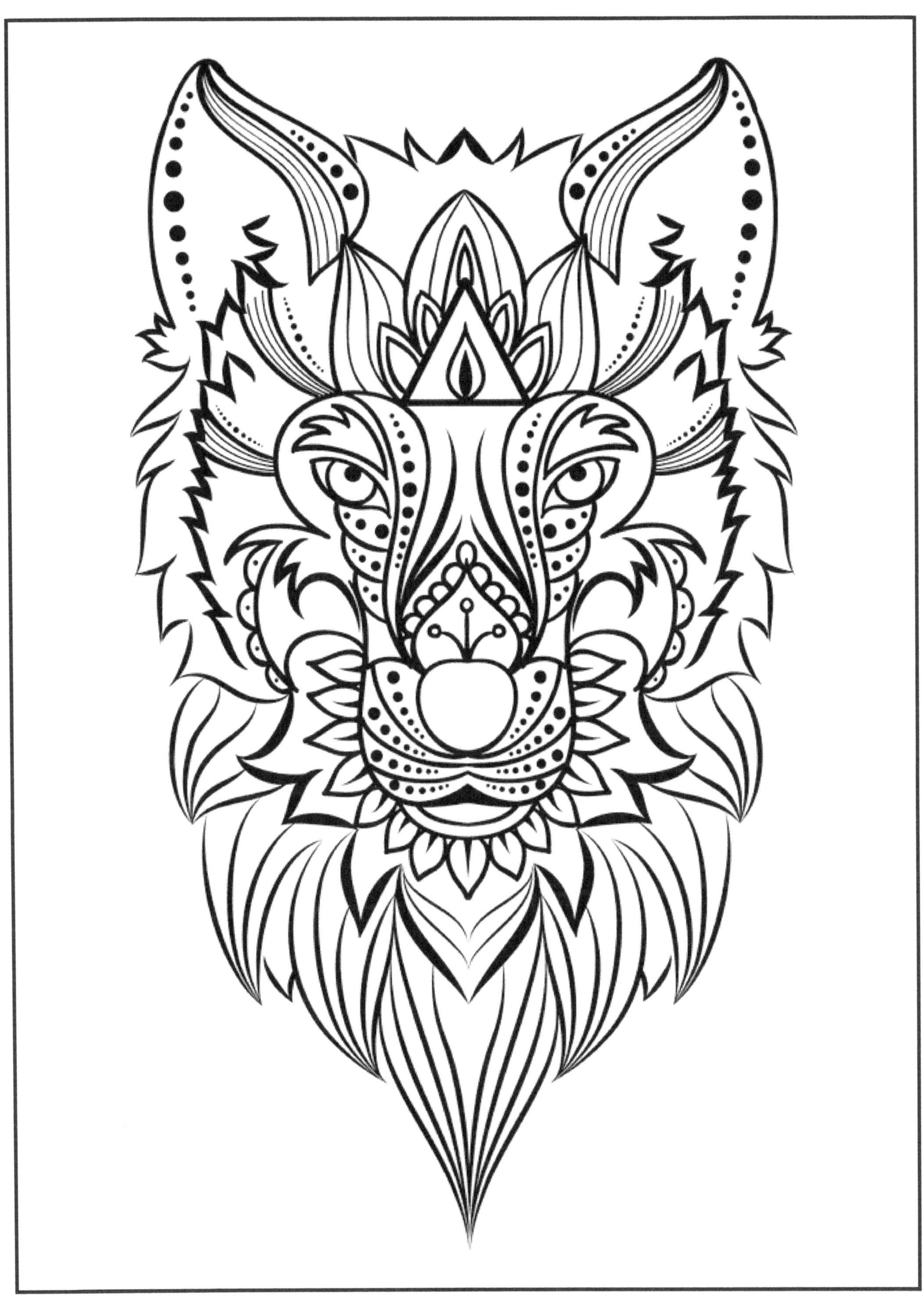

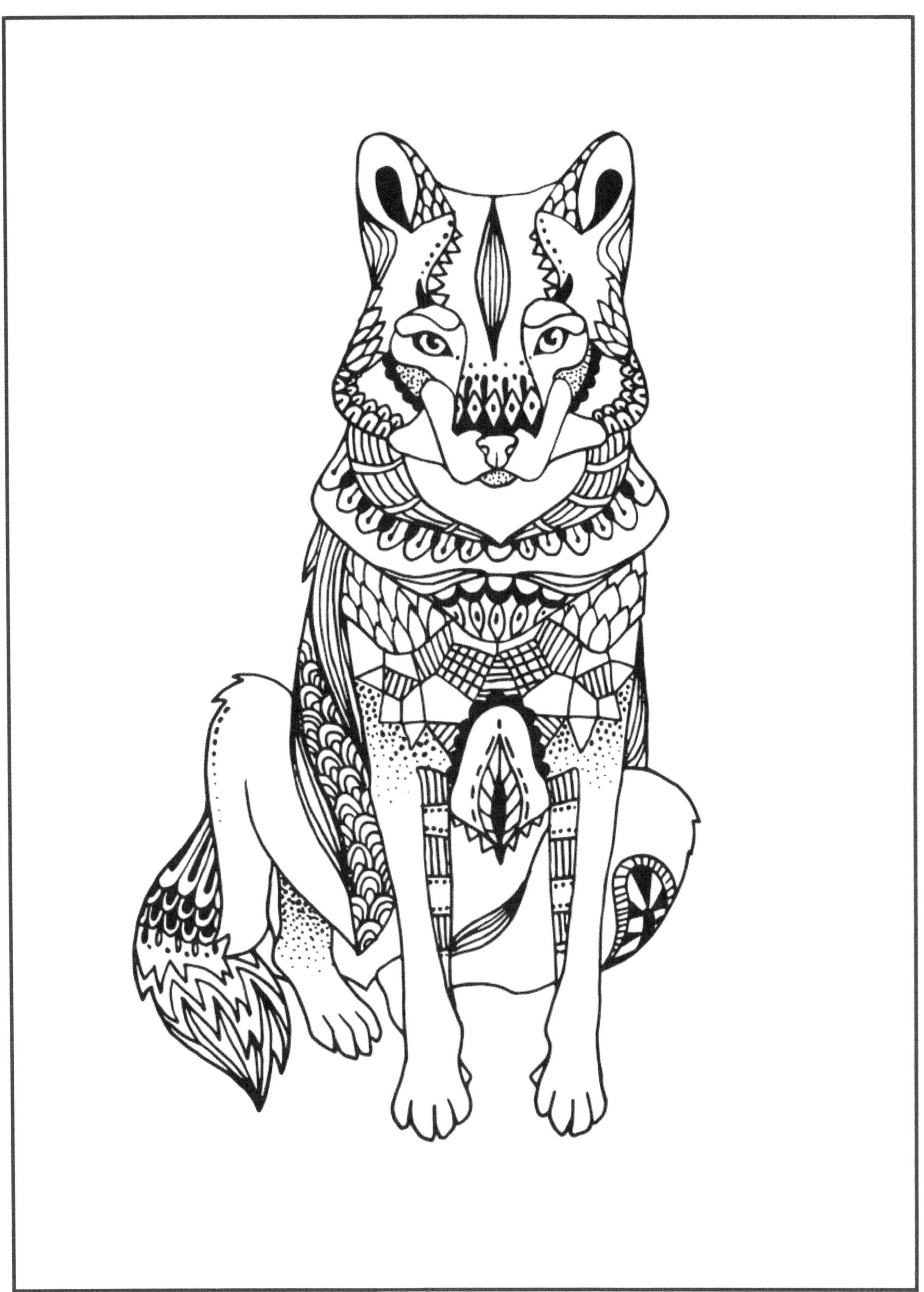

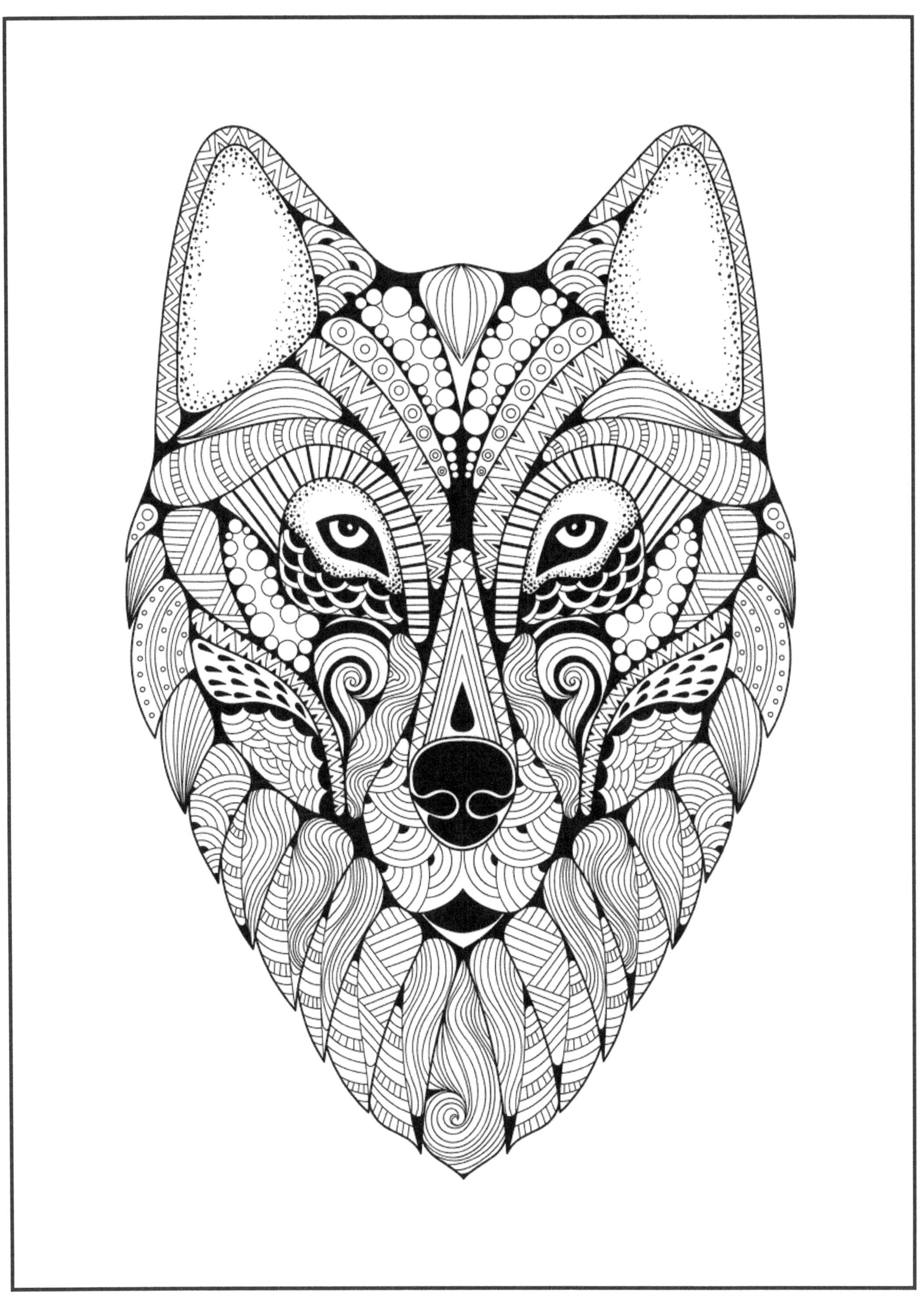

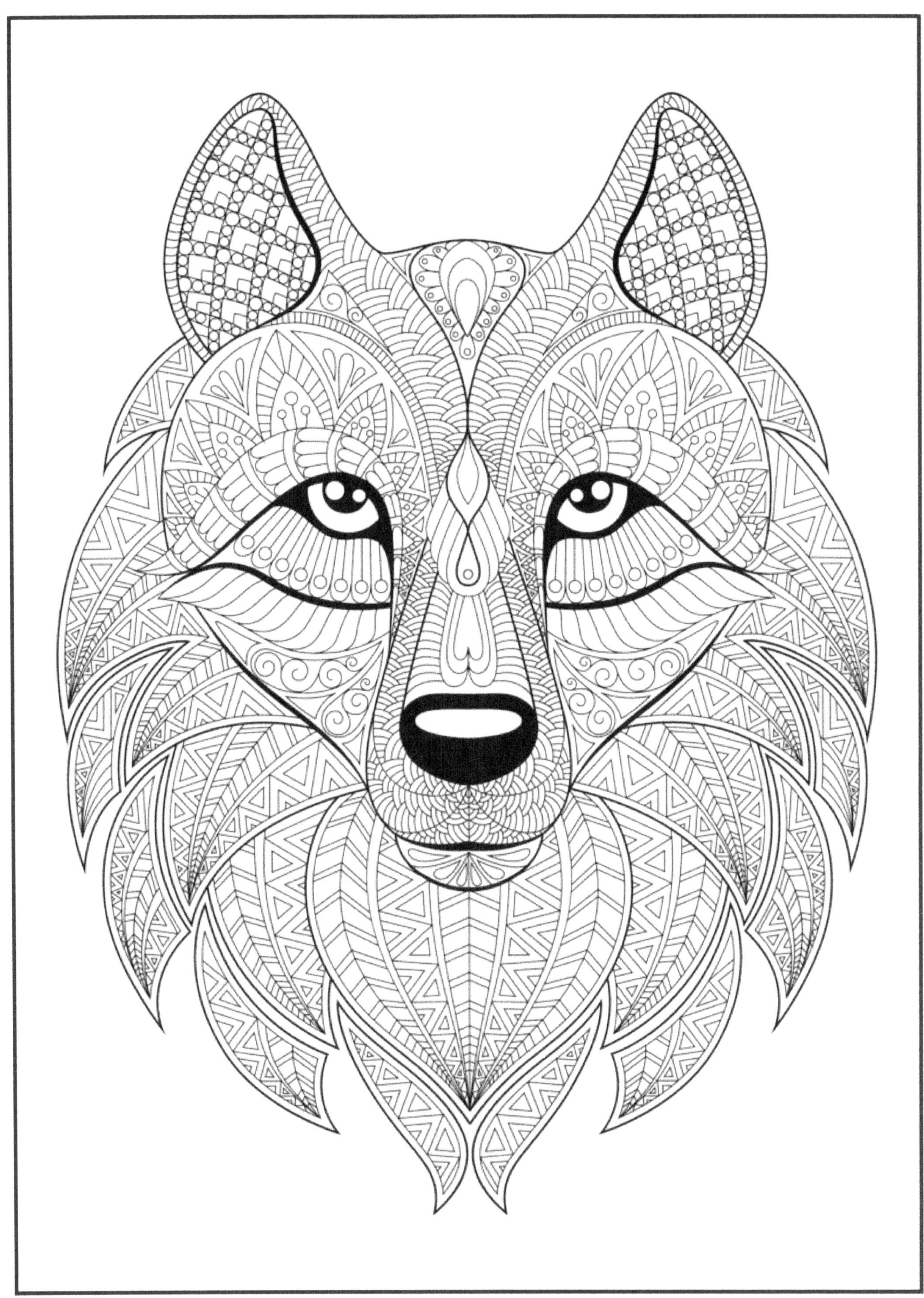

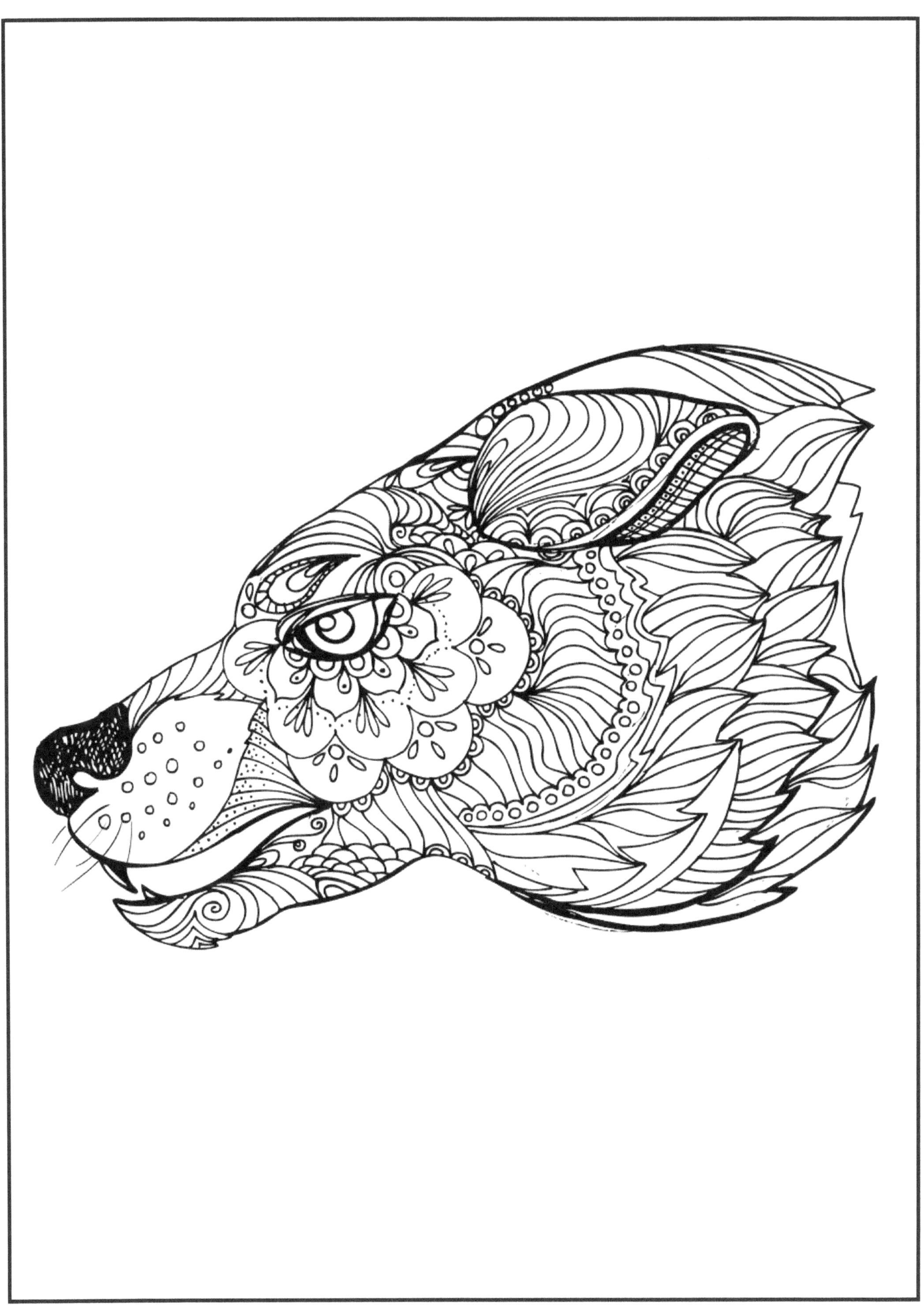

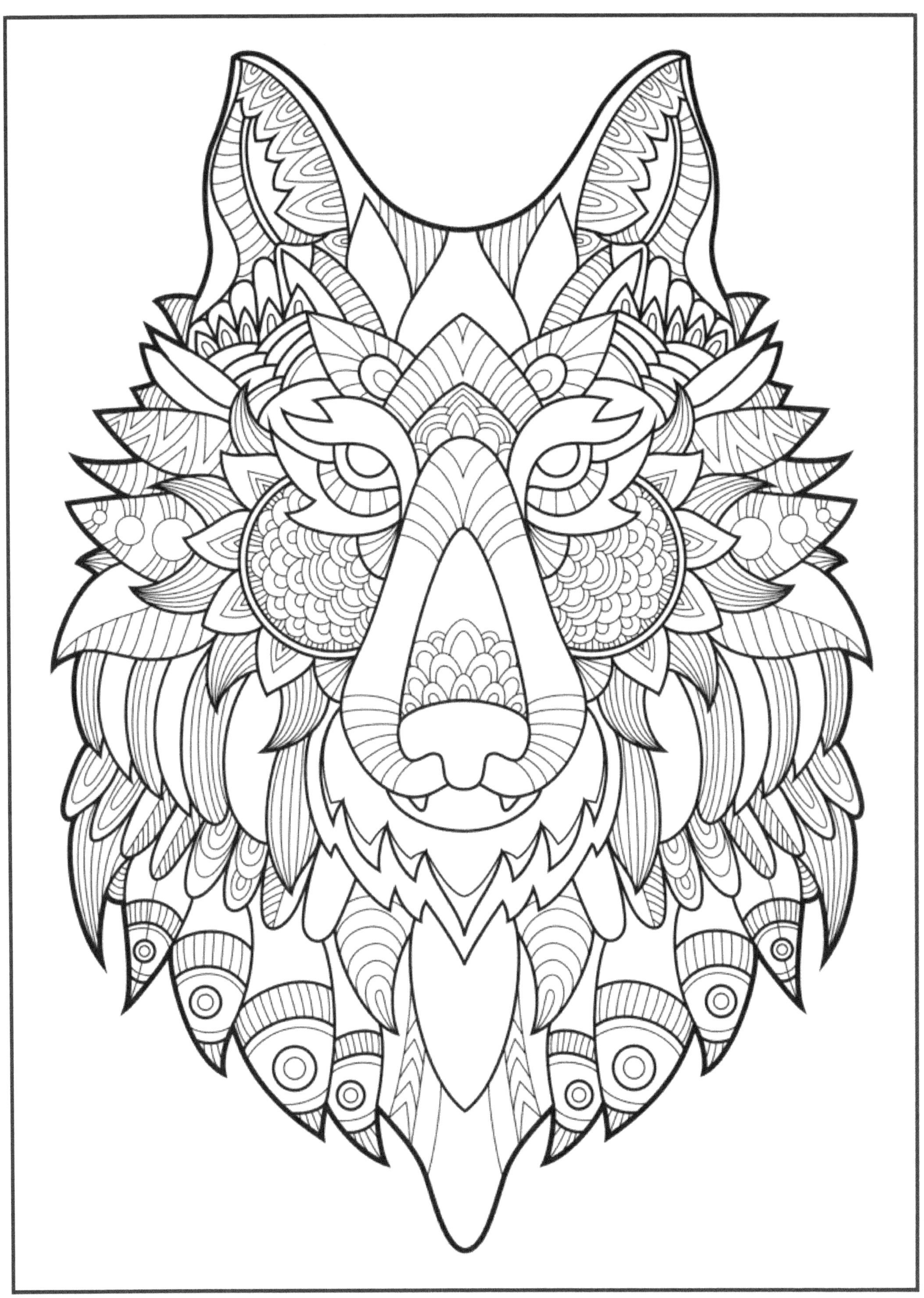

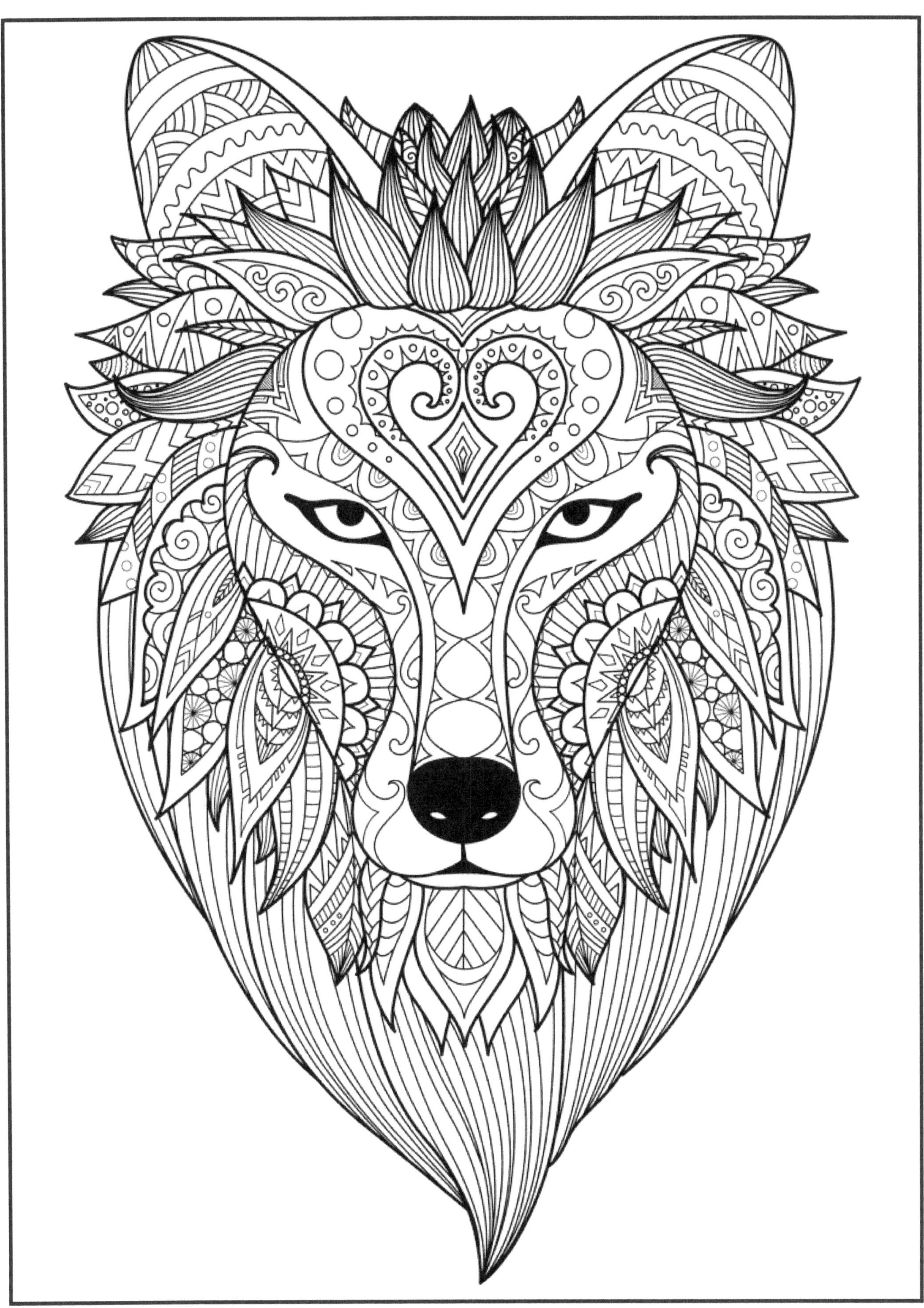

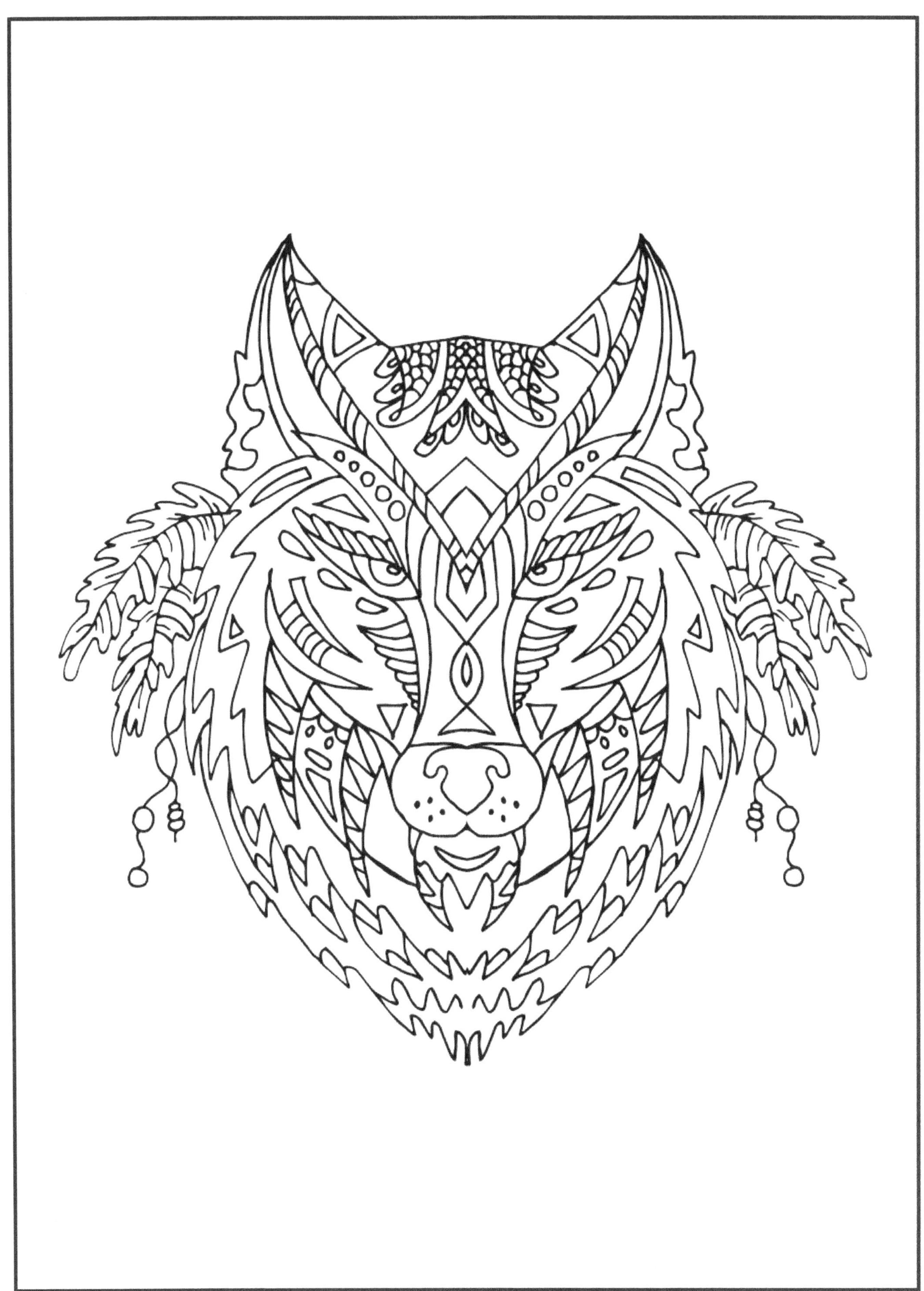

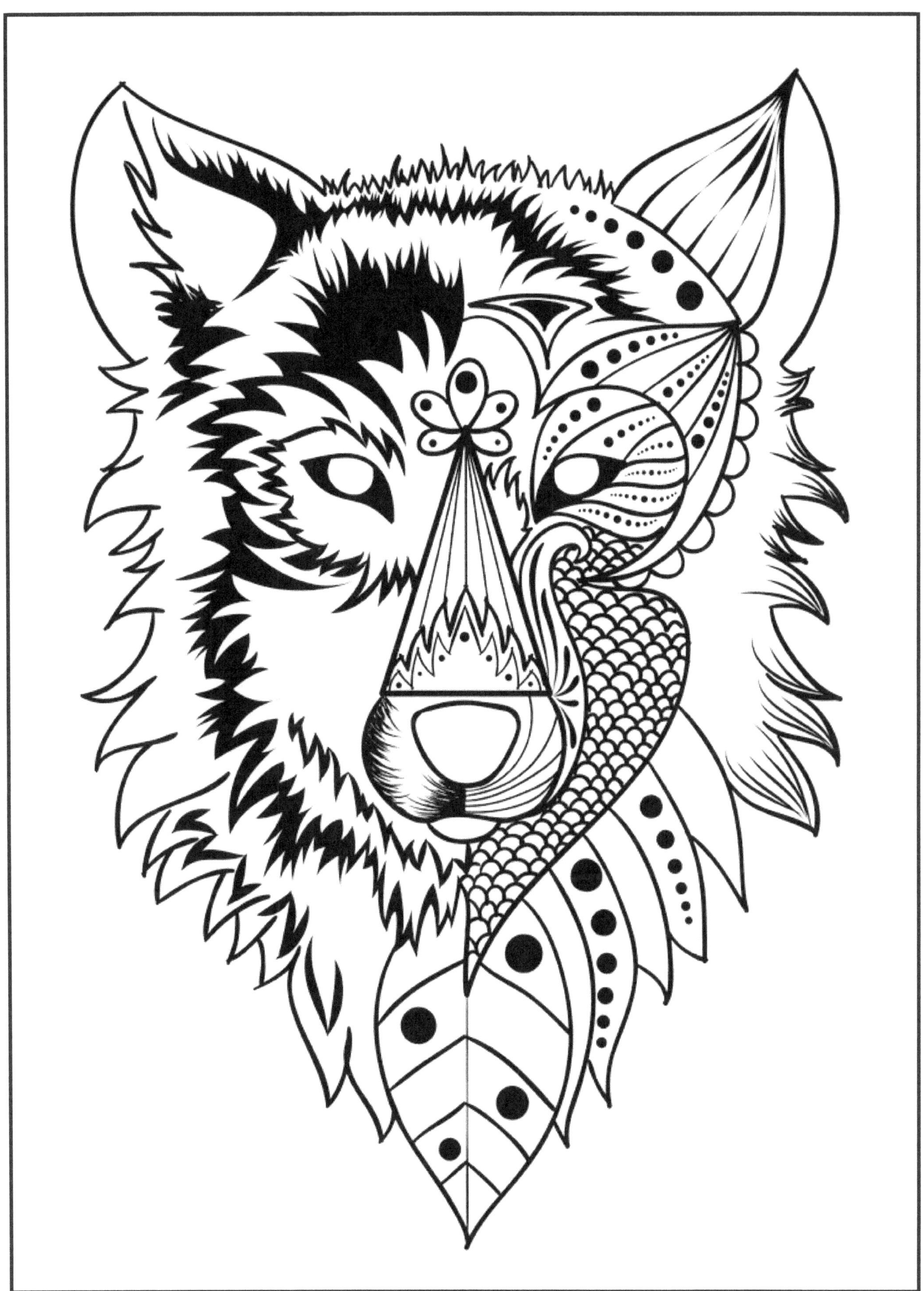

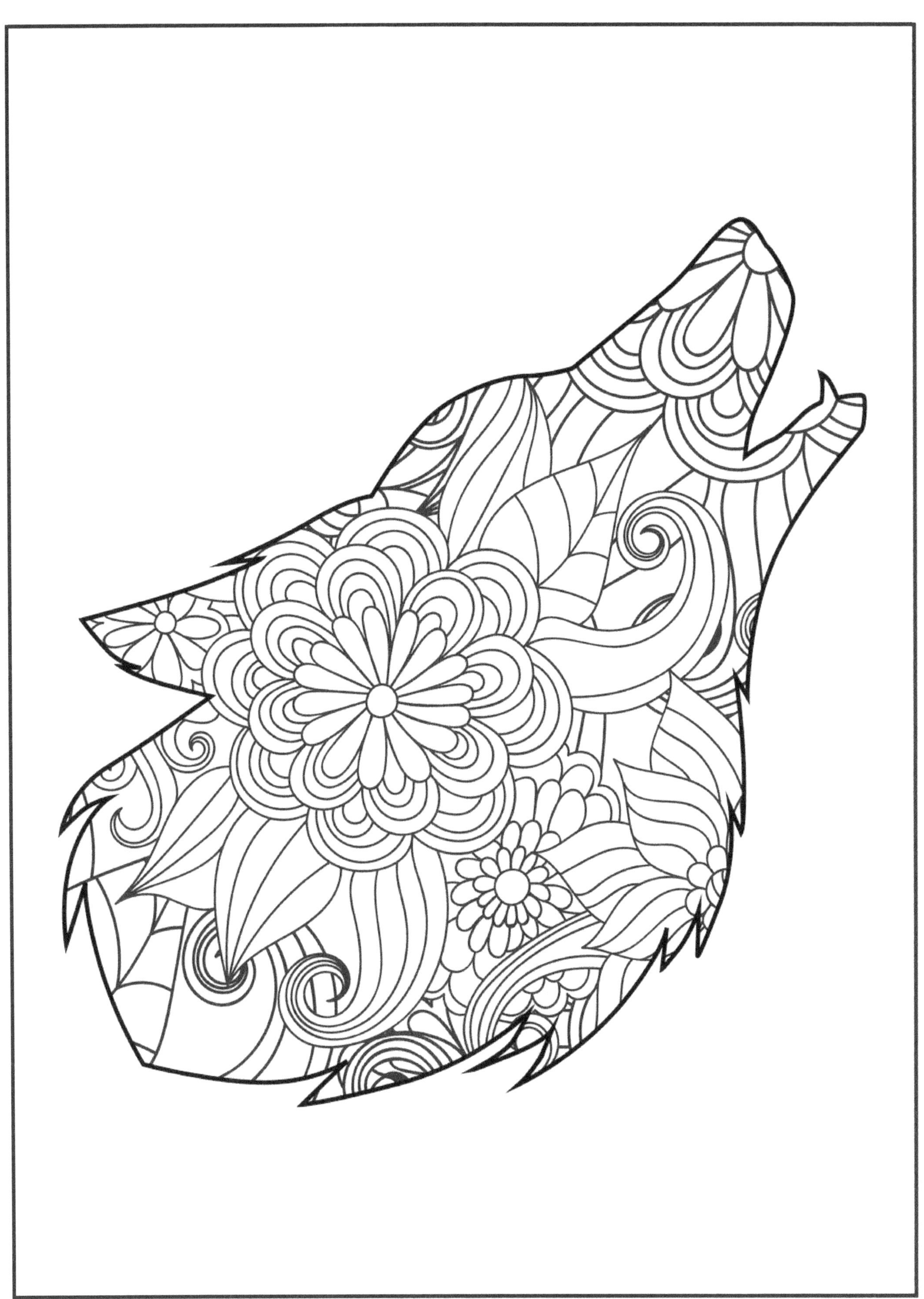

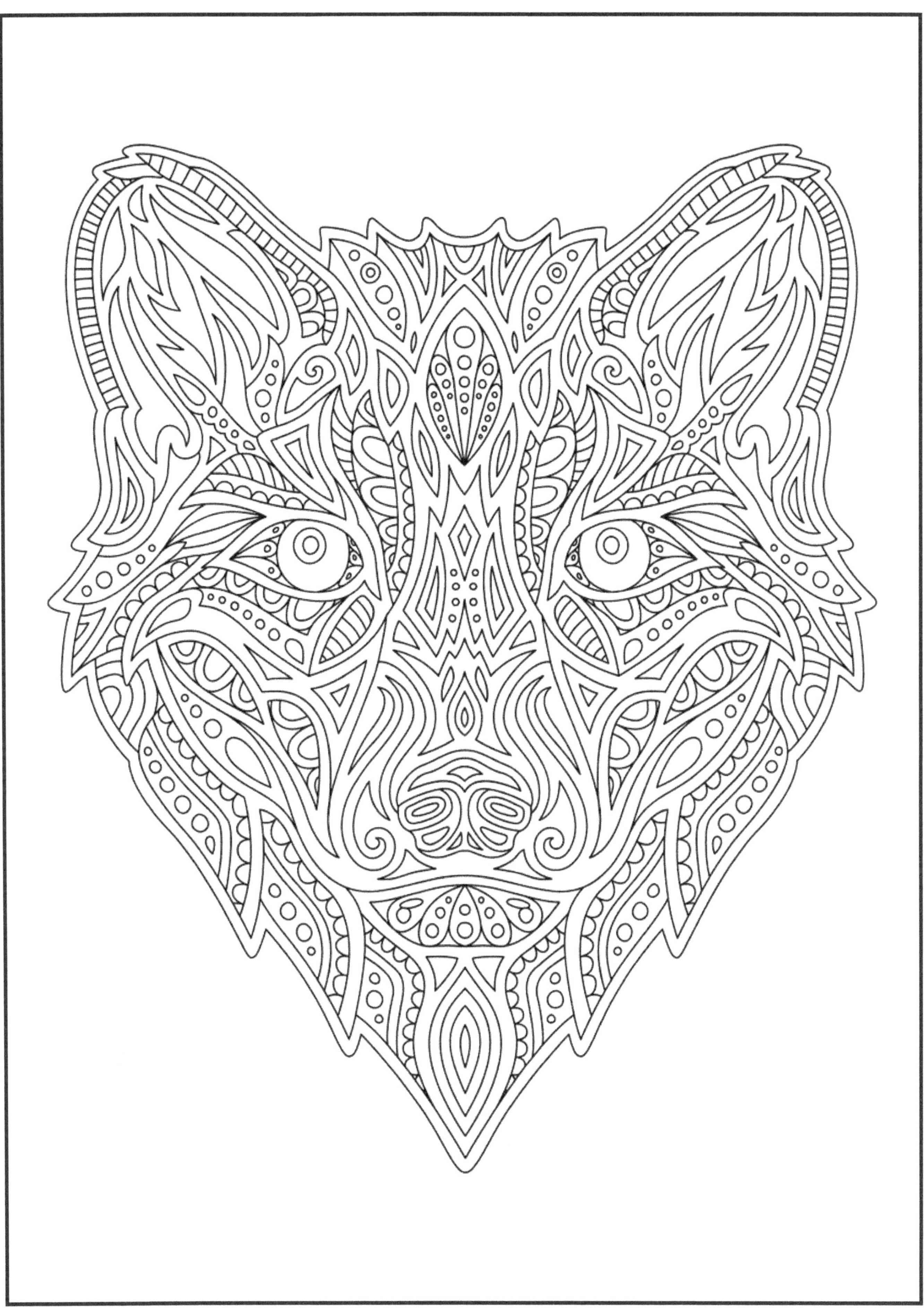

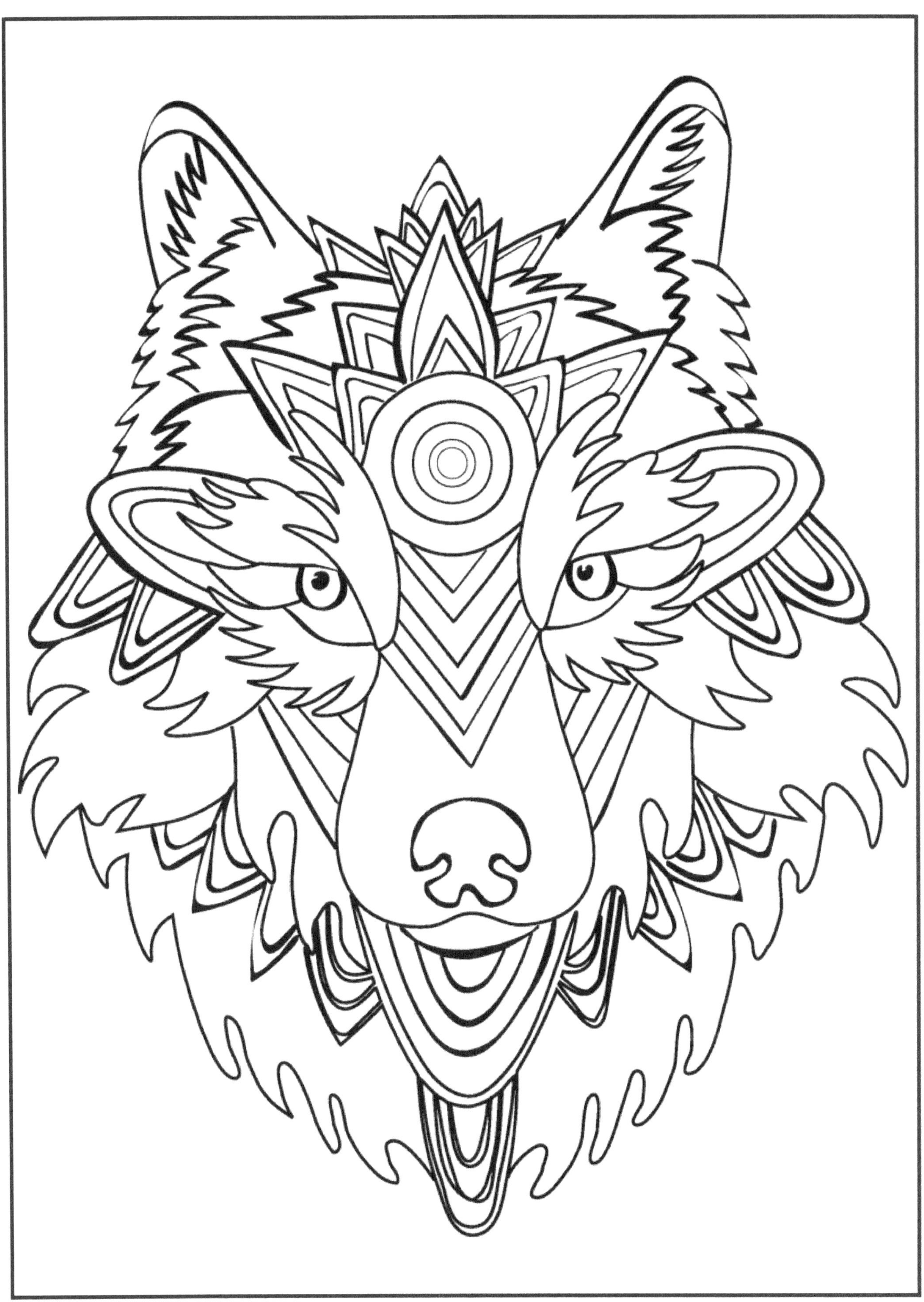

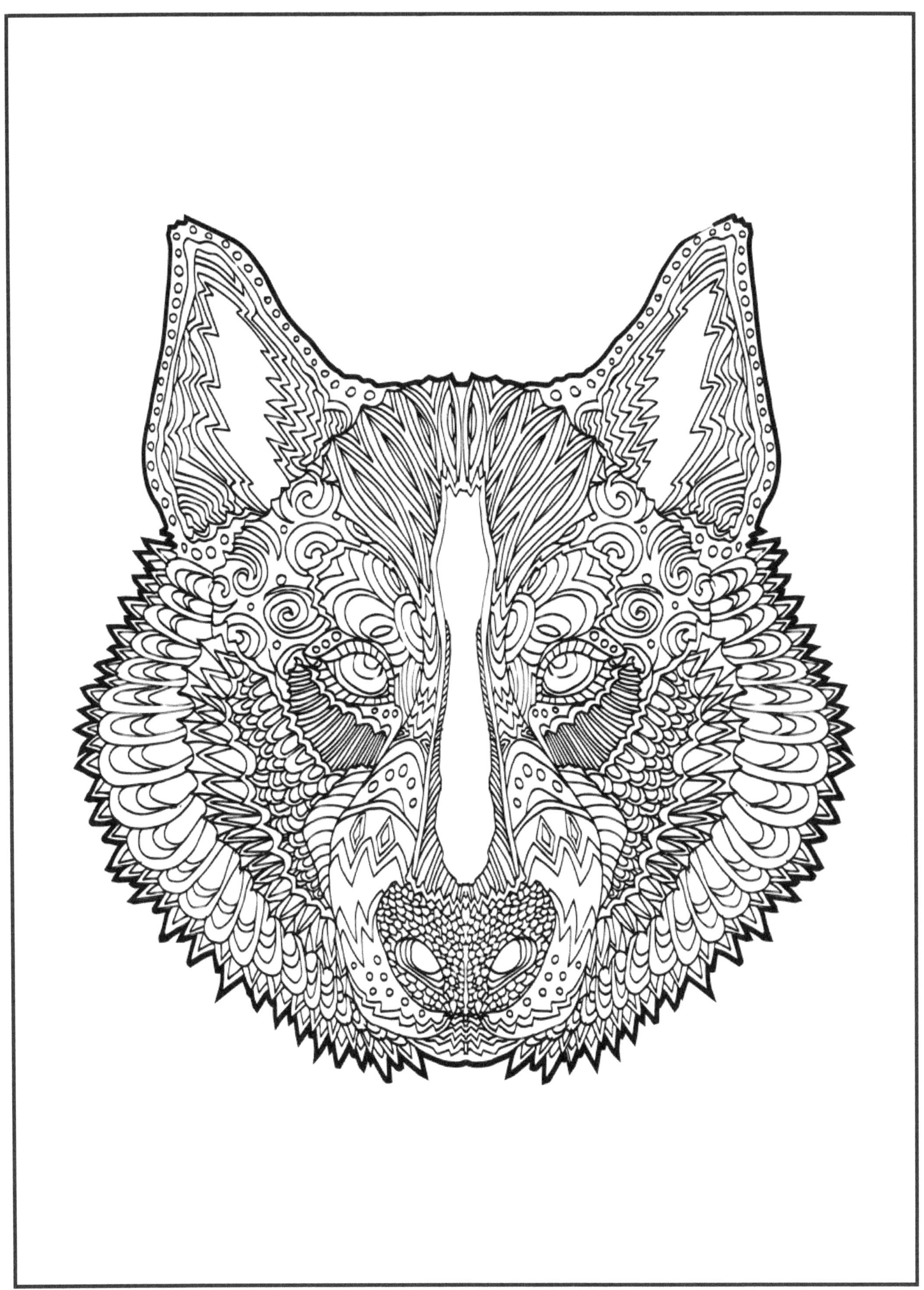

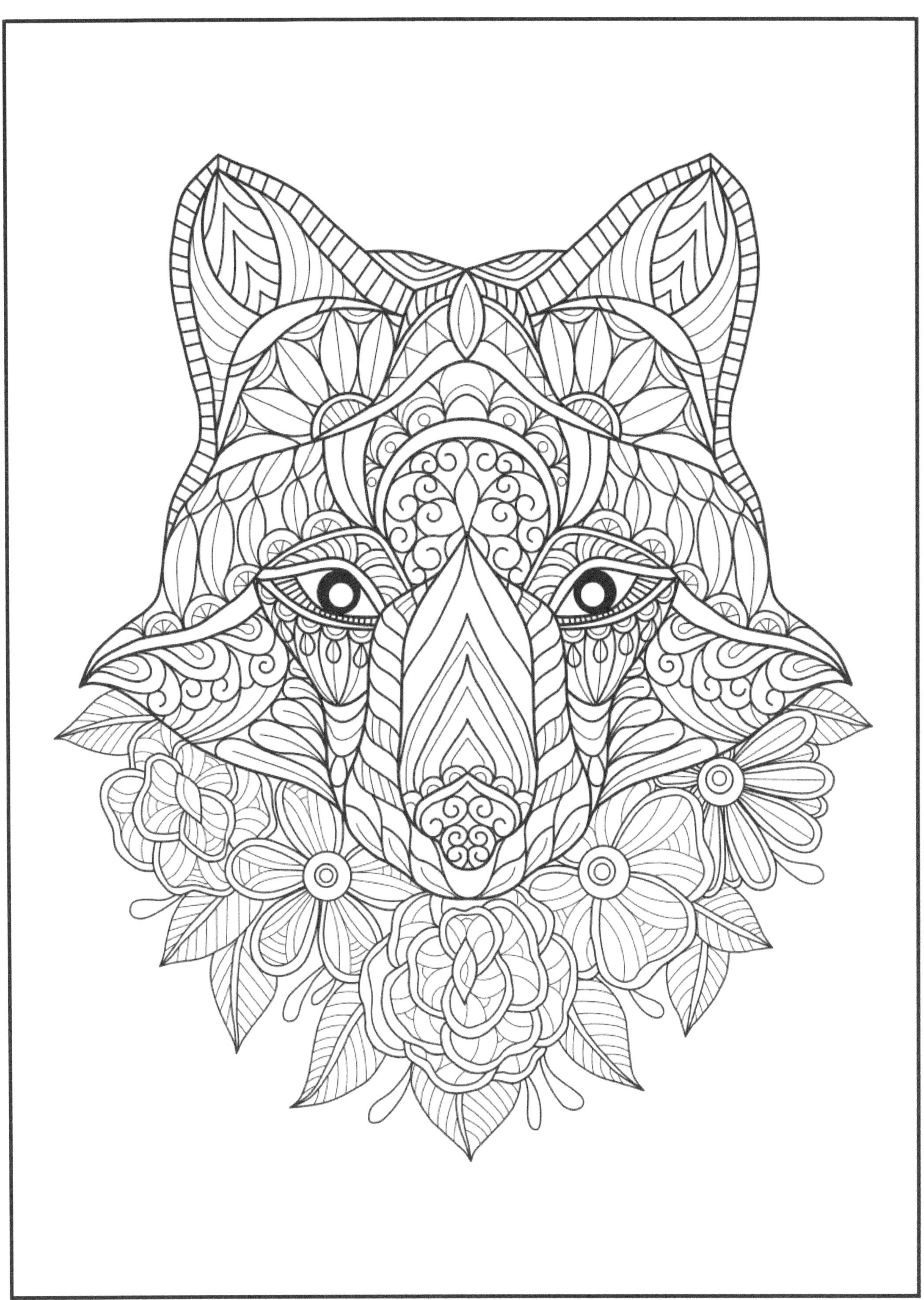

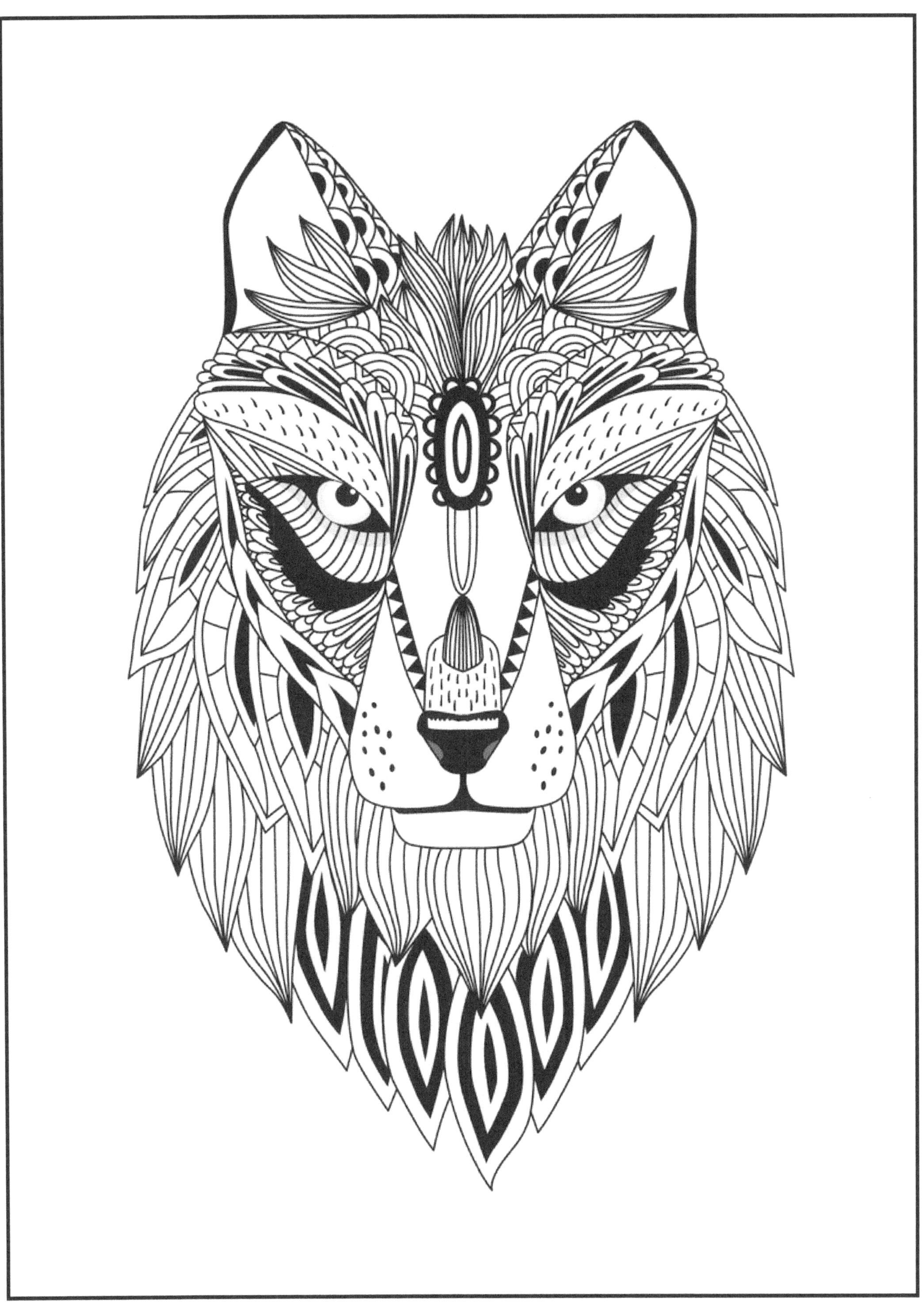

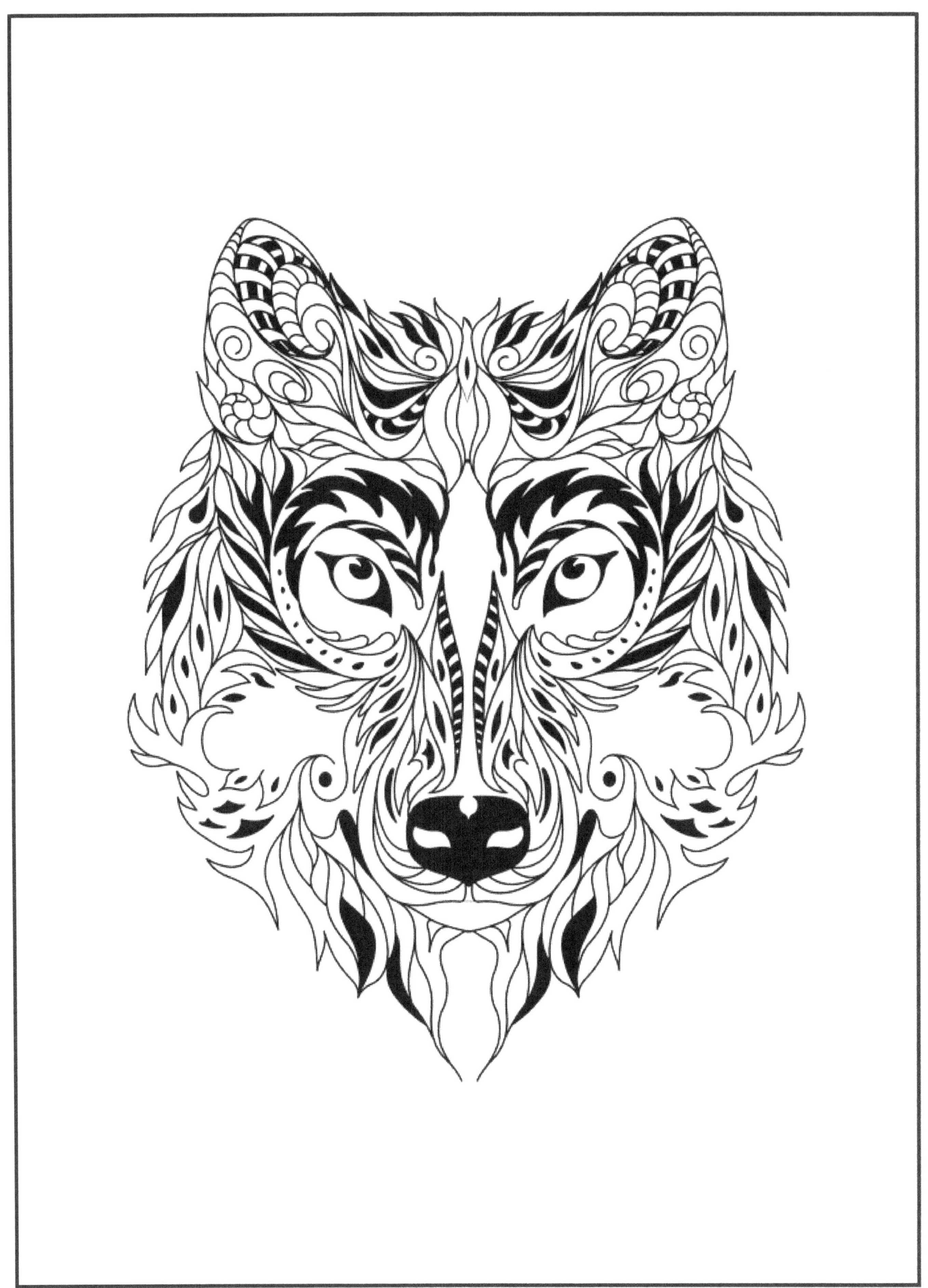

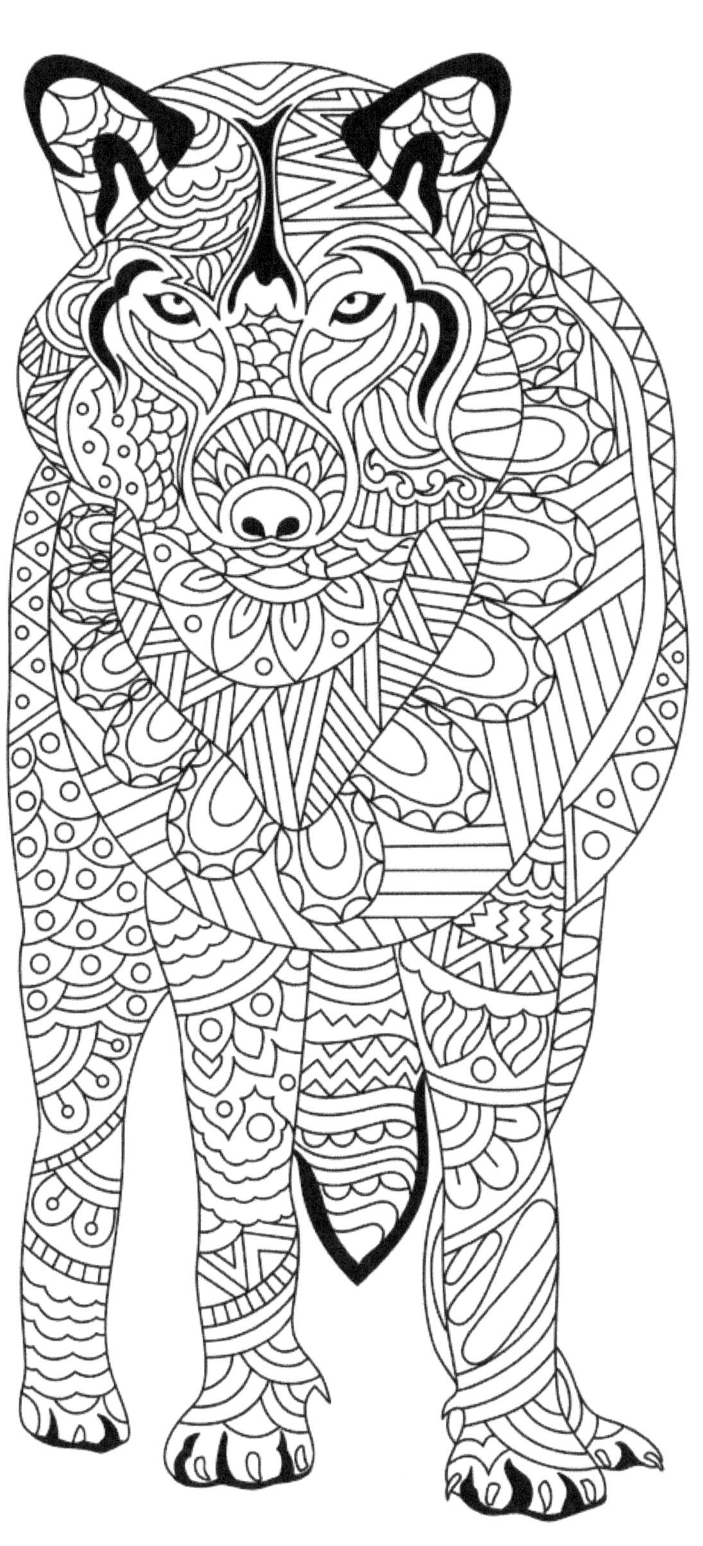

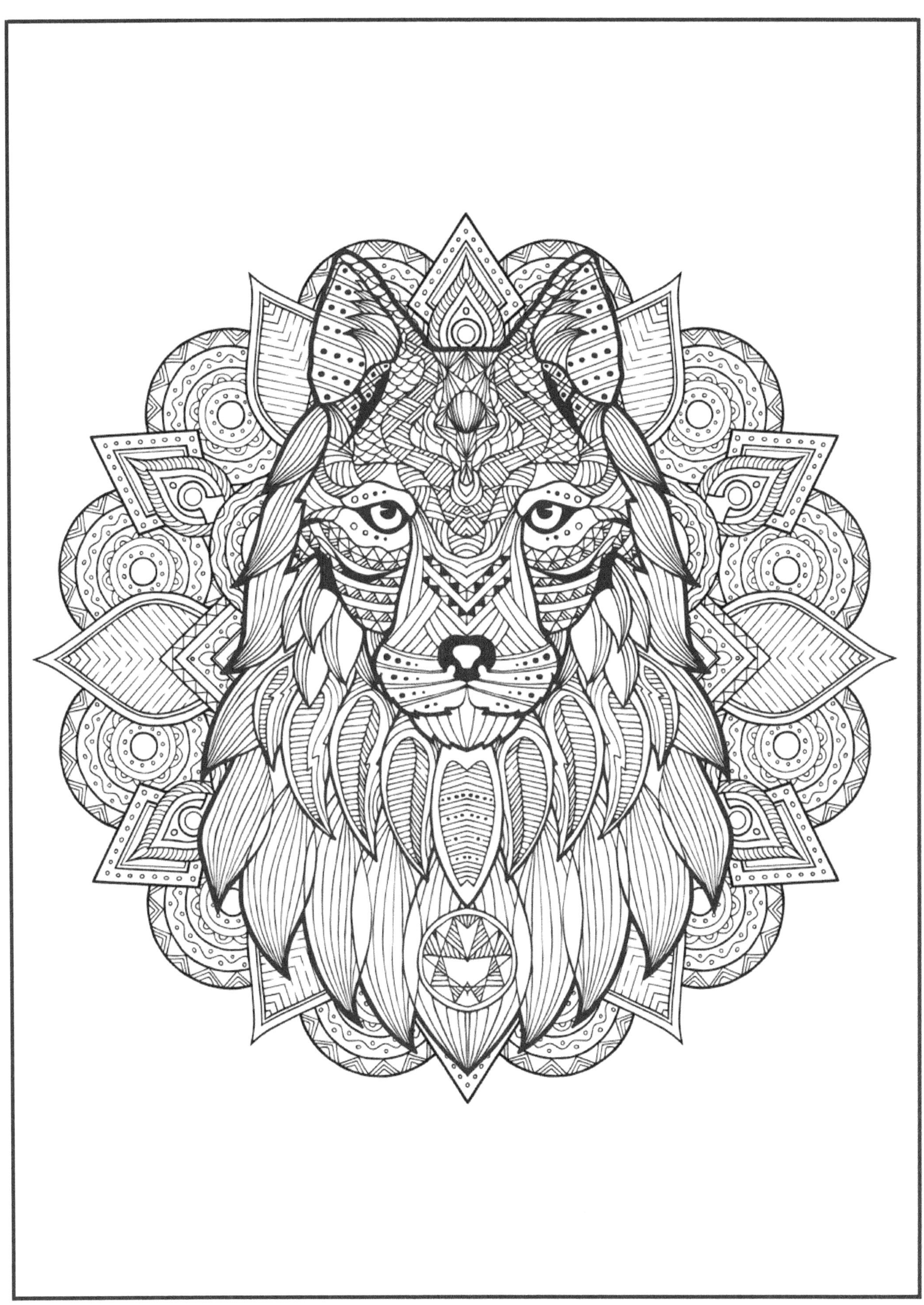

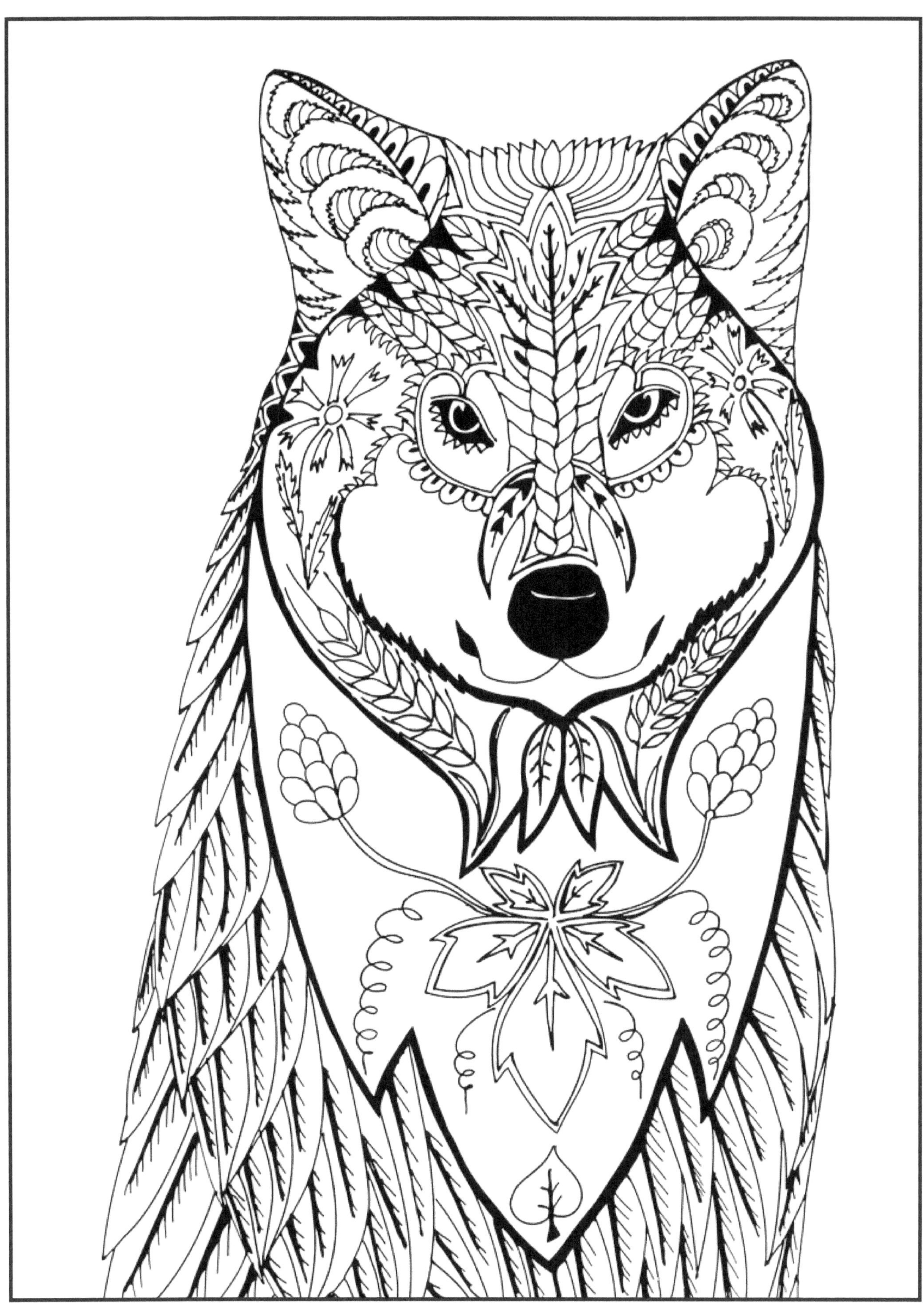

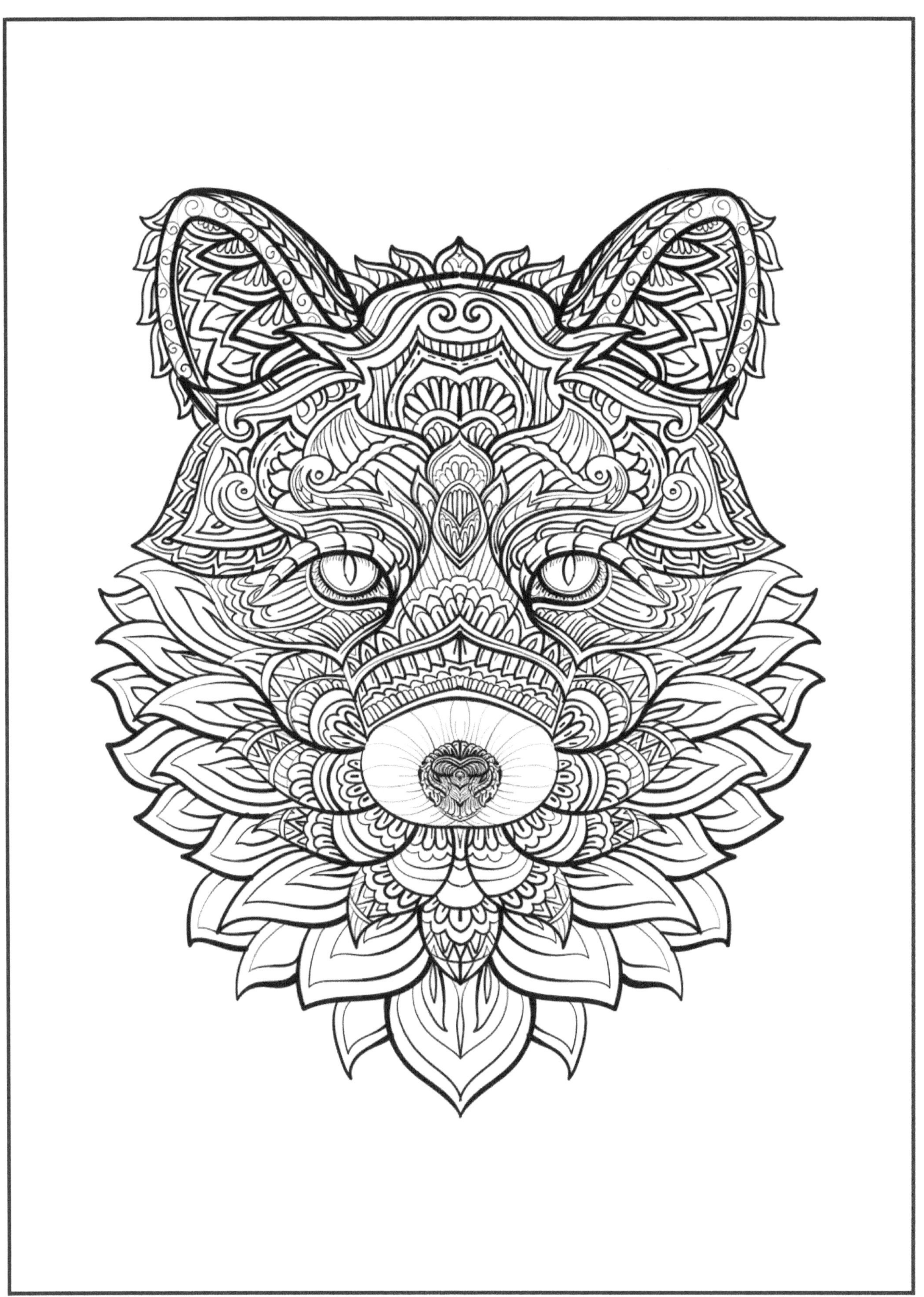

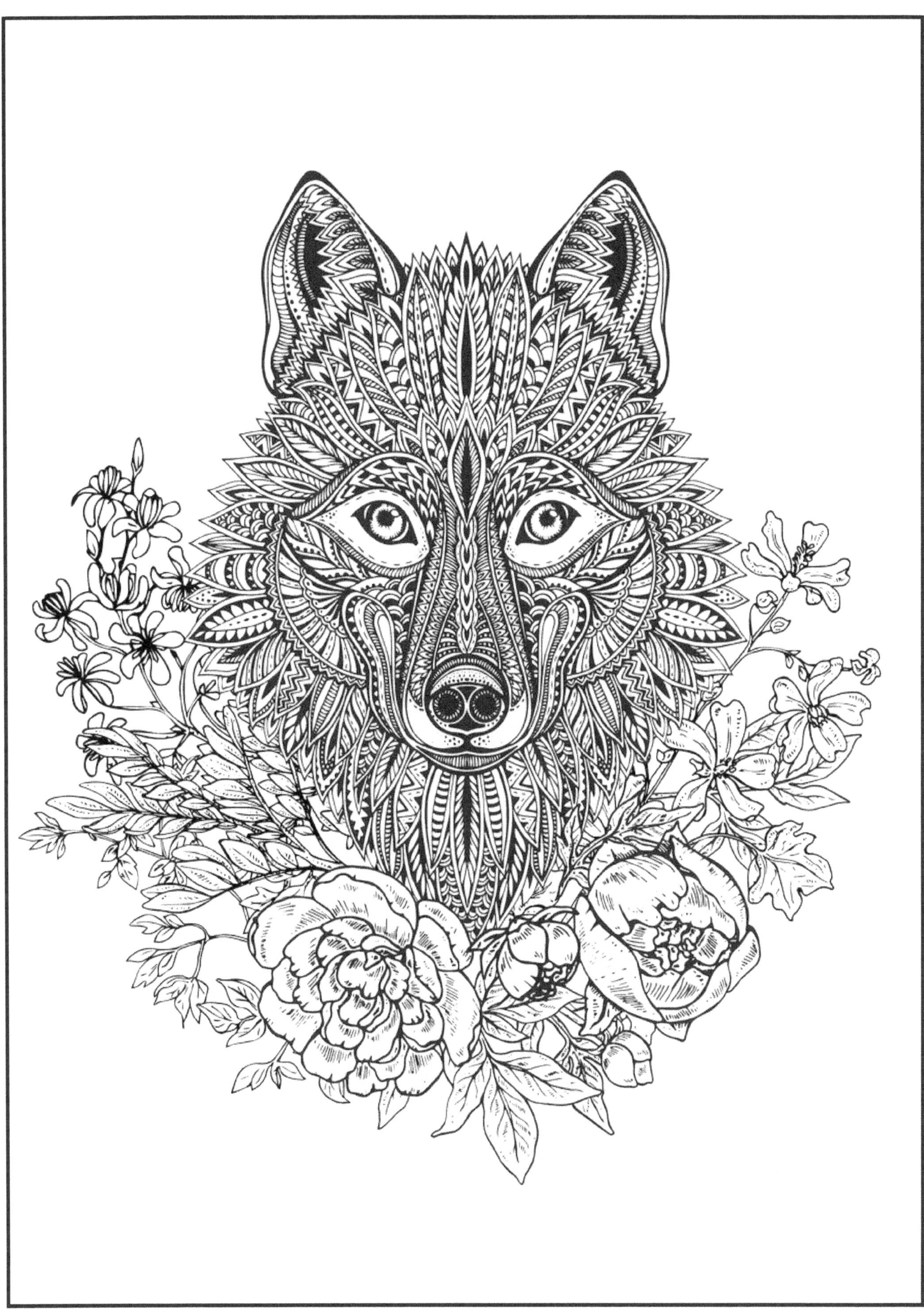

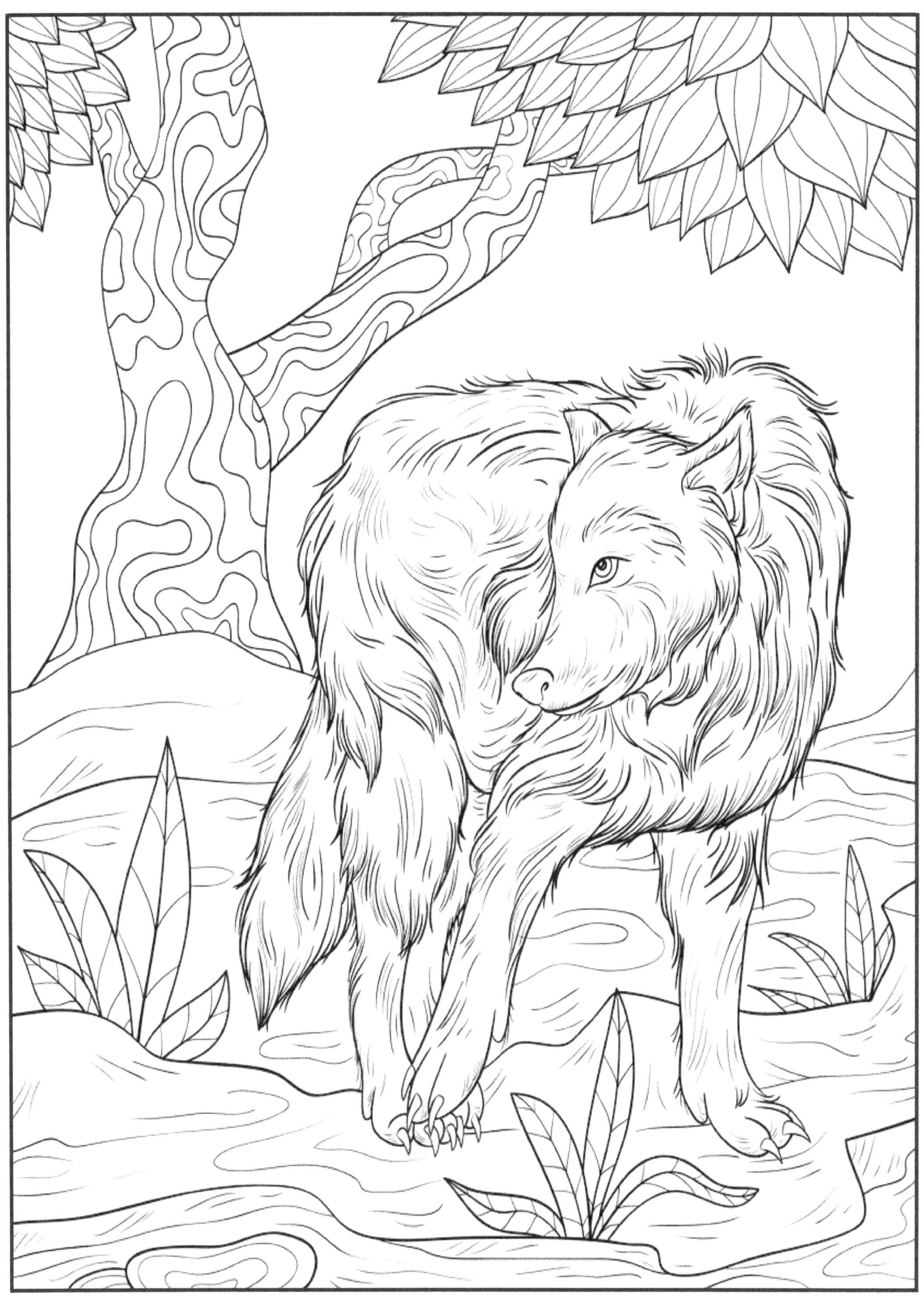

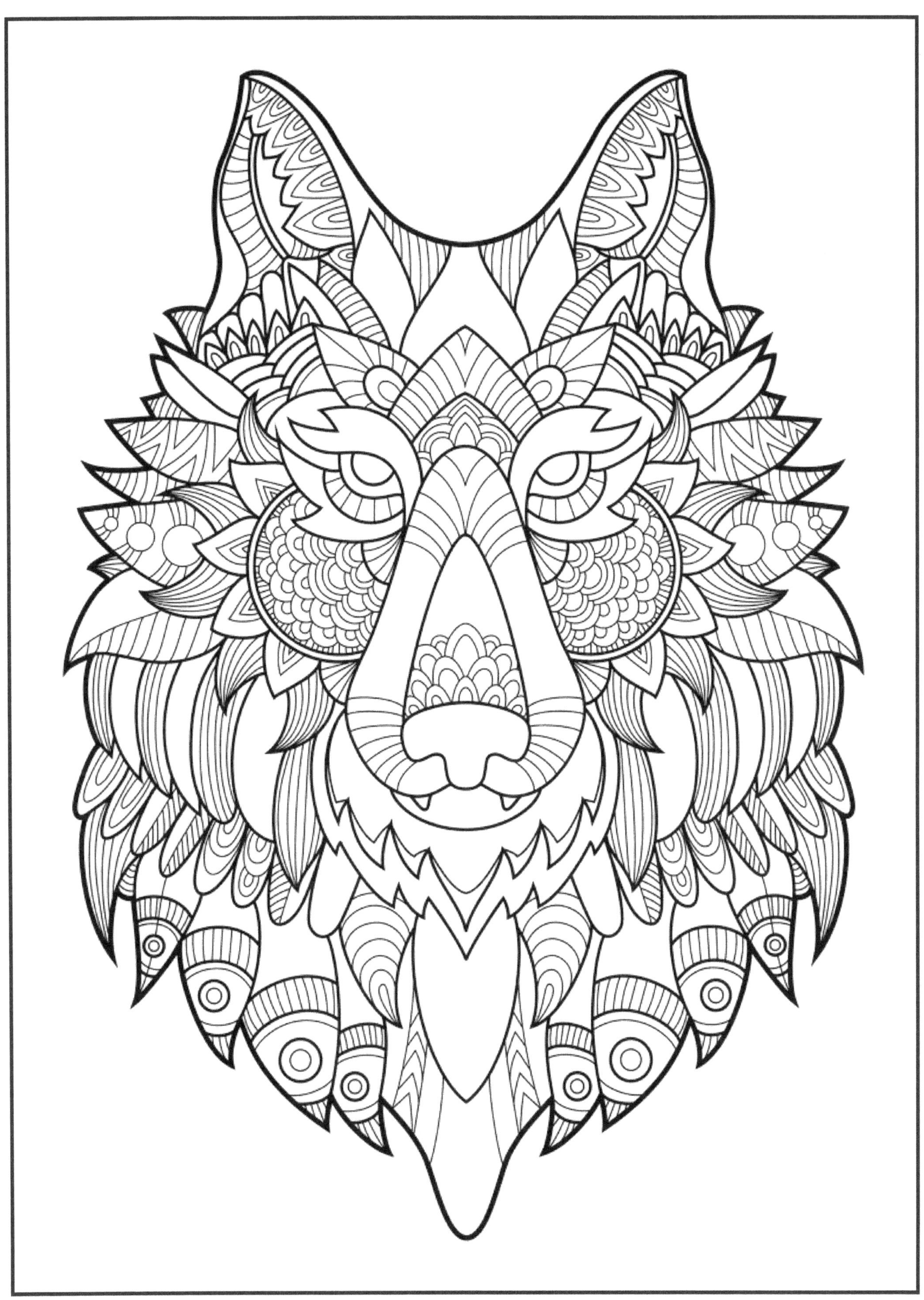

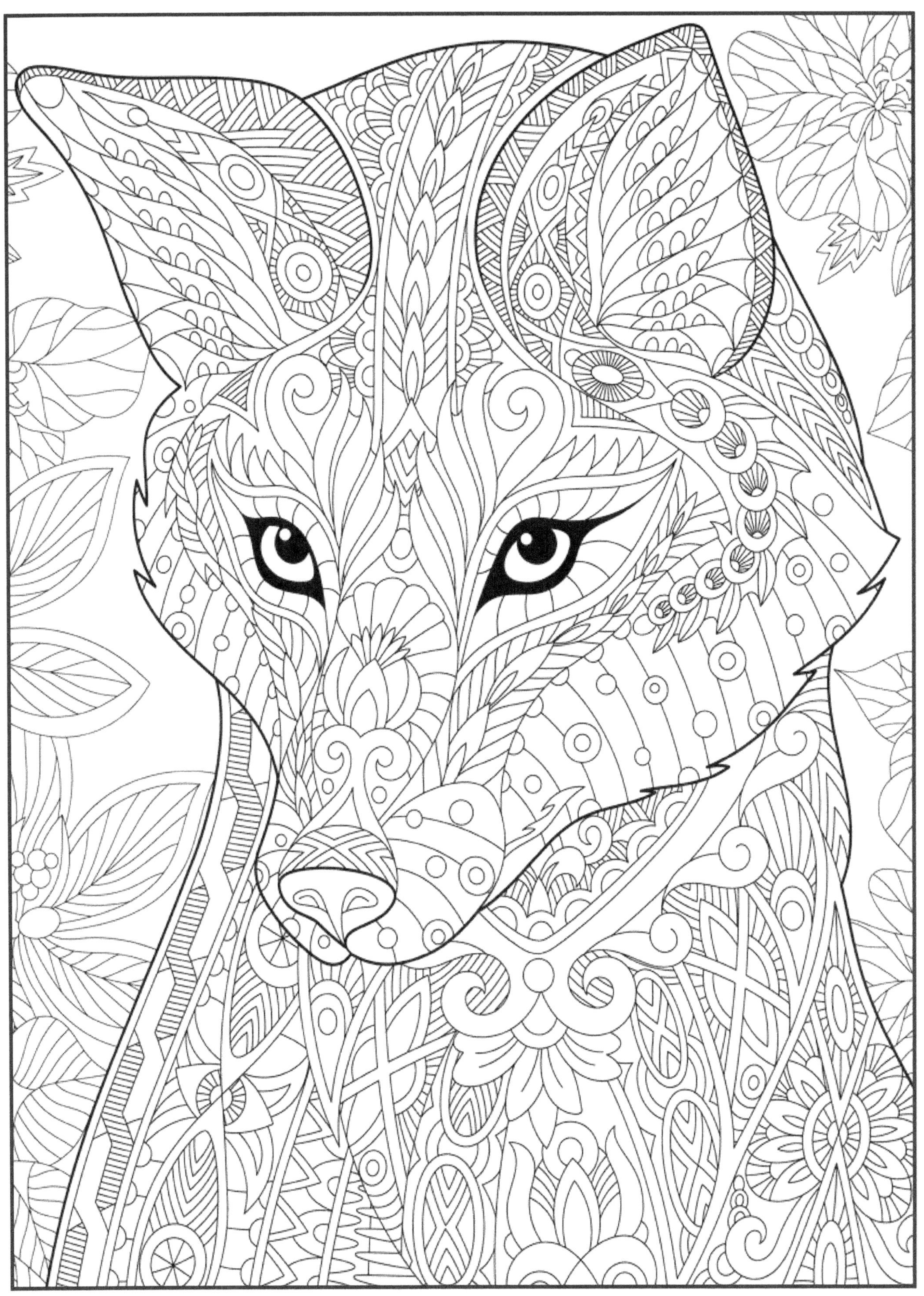

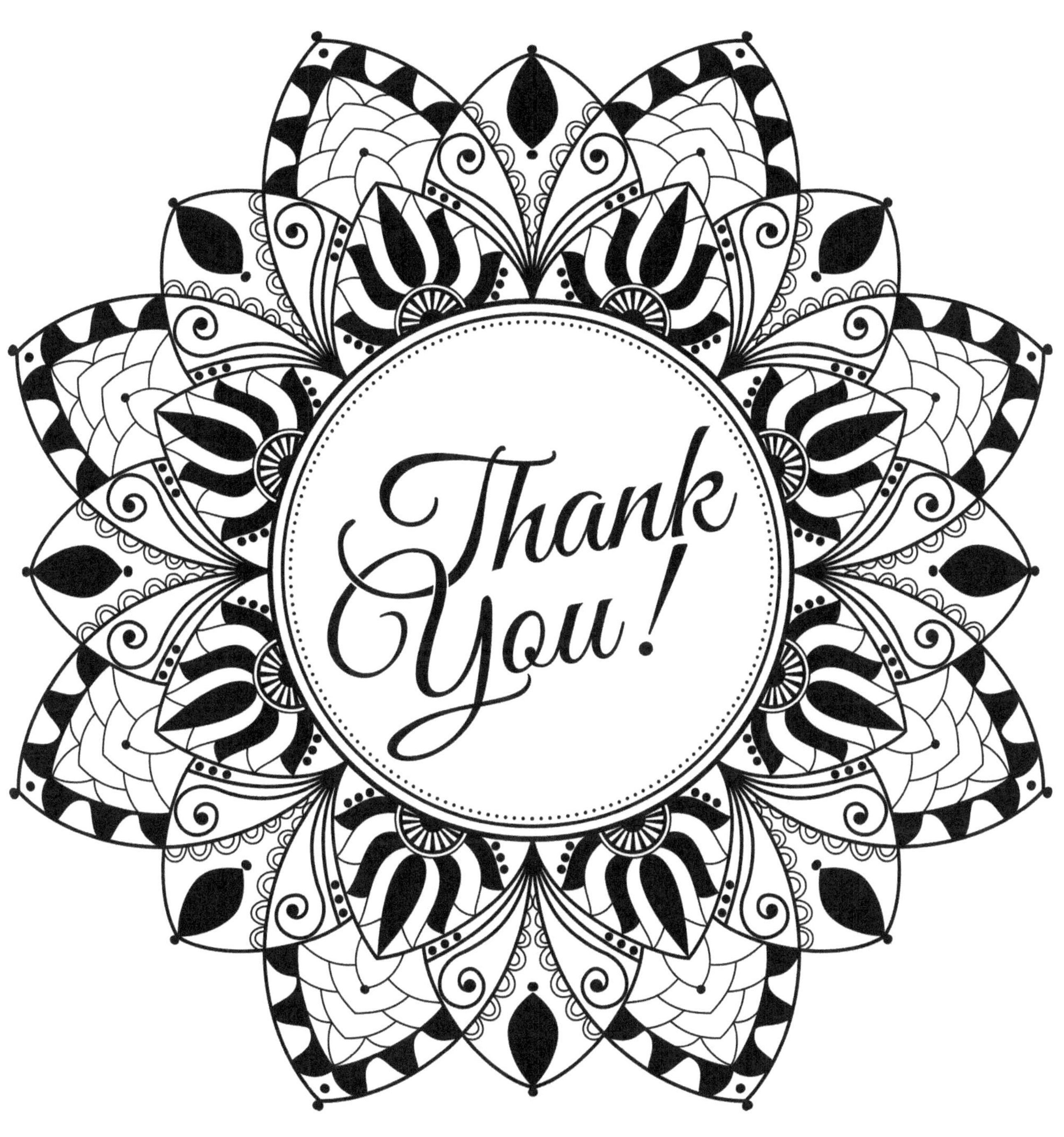

Thank You!